WORLD WAR II
NEBRASKA

★

Melissa Amateis

THE
History
PRESS

Published by The History Press
Charleston, SC
www.historypress.com

First published 2020

Manufactured in the United States

ISBN 9781467139090

Library of Congress Control Number: 2020932088

Notice: The information in this book is true and complete to the best of our knowledge. It is offered without guarantee on the part of the author or The History Press. The author and The History Press disclaim all liability in connection with the use of this book.

Dedicated to my grandparents, members of the Greatest Generation: Albert "Shorty" and Lucille Amateis and Lawrence and Aletha Bell "Lee" Woznick. Thank you for teaching me about hard work and sacrifice, but mostly, thank you for loving me unconditionally. I miss you.

CONTENTS

PREFACE

Telling the history of Nebraska during World War II simply cannot be accomplished in such a slim volume. Indeed, the complete history, as far as any history can ever be complete, would encompass dozens of volumes, if not more. In this book, I've given a brief overview of the state's major activities and accomplishments during the war years. I've sought to create a blend of academic and popular history in telling this story, although it is up to the reader to determine whether I've succeeded. Much work remains to be done on this topic, and I am hopeful that my book will spur scholars and amateur historians alike to delve further into Nebraska's World War II years.

ACKNOWLEDGEMENTS

Such a project would not be possible without the help of numerous individuals. I'd like to thank Jeff Wells, professor of history at the University of Nebraska–Kearney (UNK), for providing archival documents and photos from the Kearney Army Air Force Base; Jodi Ringbauer at the Knight Museum and Sandhills Center in Alliance, Nebraska, for help with photos (and our shared love for Geronimo, the incredible parachuting dog!) of the Alliance Air Base; James Griffin, director/curator at the Lincoln County Historical Museum in North Platte, Nebraska, for help with North Platte Canteen photos; Hannah Palsa for generously sharing her archival documents on Fort Robinson's K-9 dog training; David Wolf, executive director of the Legacy of the Plains Museum in Gering, Nebraska, for photos of the Scottsbluff Air Base (and Jordyn for scanning them); Elizabeth Spilinek from the Adams County Historical Society for her assistance with photos from the Hastings Naval Ammunition Depot; Katie Nieland for graphics and image help; my History Press acquisitions editor, Artie Crisp, for being so patient and understanding throughout this entire process; Randy Bright for photo help and for being an awesome friend; my co-workers for their support; and my friends Nancy Harter, Don Robertson, Alexis Radil, Janna Leadbetter, Scott Patterson, Jereme Haden and Stephen Johnston for being there for me, for celebrating and commiserating and for just generally being awesome people. Special thanks to my significant other, Johnie, for your unwavering support and devotion; my family for their love and support; and extra special thanks to my daughter, Molly, for putting up with a preoccupied mother for the past two years and for loving history just as much as I do.

INTRODUCTION

I n December 1941, the Empire of Japan attacked the U.S. naval base at Pearl Harbor in Hawaii, and America suddenly plunged into another world war. The country's isolationists fell silent as reports came of the destruction of U.S. naval destroyers and nearly three thousand American casualties, the first of many for the United States. Some of those casualties were from Nebraska. The war "over there" in the countries of Europe and the nations of the Far East touched Nebraskans and every other American.

The attack on Pearl Harbor produced a thirst for revenge against Japan, and when Germany declared war on the United States, the German-American Bund became all but irrelevant. Charles Lindbergh and his America First group dissolved. With the exception of a few who clung to the fringes, America was united behind President Roosevelt when he declared a state of war against the Axis powers.

Nebraskans answered the call in every way possible. Men and women joined the military forces; the U.S. military placed three ordnance plants and two naval munitions depot in the state; Nebraska farmers pitched in to help feed not only America but also soldiers overseas; Henry Doorly's scrap drive, known as the "Nebraska Plan," became the model for a nationwide scrap drive; eleven air bases dotted the state from east to west; United Service Organizations (USOs) and war bond drives and victory gardens appeared; war dogs were trained at Fort Robinson; and B-29 planes were built at the Martin Bomber Plant at Fort Crook, Nebraska.

In late 1943, Axis prisoners captured in North Africa came to Nebraska, the first of many, and became integral to closing the labor gap left by the men off fighting. The North Platte Canteen welcomed soldiers from all across America and made their journey a little bit more special with birthday cakes and fried chicken, plus a hefty dose of hometown hospitality. A Nebraska Nisei joined the U.S. Army Air Forces and faced prejudice and racism. Likewise, black soldiers faced racism and bigotry in the workforce of the Hastings Naval Ammunition Depot and as airmen in the U.S. Army Air Forces bases scattered around Nebraska. Women left to work at the Cornhusker Plant, the POW camps, the factories and anywhere else they were needed. Children played war on sunny afternoons as they looked for scrap and listened to the FBI radio program as the G-Men hunted for Nazi saboteurs. Citizens worked in tandem with the military and factories located in their communities, creating a symbiotic relationship whose effects reverberated far into the future.

The war touched every part of life, and when it was over in 1945, Nebraska would never be the same again. Despite being largely isolationist before the Pearl Harbor attack, Nebraskans answered the call for war, becoming an invaluable and critical part of America's fight to win World War II.

Chapter 1

WAR COMES TO NEBRASKA

Long before the attack on Pearl Harbor in December 1941, America watched the war in Europe with bated breath. The last time the United States participated in a global war, thousands of American lives were lost, and this deadly conflict with Hitler and Mussolini only promised more of the same. For years, isolationism, partly fueled by the despair and anger of the Great Depression, divided the country, manifesting in organizations like the America First Party with famous aviator Charles Lindbergh a vocal proponent. Some German Americans, still smarting from their persecution during World War I, gladly supported Hitler's Nazi Party and joined the German-American Bund. Most, however, were vocal in their opposition to Nazi Germany and fiercely loyal to America, the country that had given them refuge and welcome.

Other Americans found sanctuary with far-right groups that embraced fascism, anti-Semitism and white nationalism. Small pockets of these groups even popped up in Nebraska—Omaha resident and anti-Semite Charles B. Hudson wrote and published a propaganda-filled tract called America in Danger! that peddled conspiracy theories, decried communism and embraced Christian nationalism.[1] There were German-American Bund members in Nebraska, but their numbers were small. For the most part, Nebraskans had little to do with these outliers. Yet as sensational headlines spread across the country about the German-American Bund's "Pro-America" rally—which was really a pro-Nazi rally—in New York City's Madison Square Garden on February 20, 1939, many Americans were outraged and worried. Rumors of possible Fifth Columnists already poised to take down America from within also set off alarm bells. But the majority of Americans, including the majority of Nebraskans, preferred to take a wait-and-see approach. Not many were eager to enter the war. Some in Congress, especially Nebraska representatives, wanted the United States to stay out of Europe's problems. Many of their constituents agreed. No need to send American boys to once again die on the battlefields of Europe.

Despite this hesitancy, Nebraska senator Edward R. Burke introduced a bill in Congress for a peacetime draft. Numerous Great Plains residents opposed it, as well as Nebraska senator George Norris, a well-known isolationist who had also opposed America's entry into World War I. Nevertheless, the Selective Training and Service Act passed on September 16, 1940.[2]

America was inching ever closer to being involved in "Europe's problems," even though most of the American people had no wish to be. In a Gallup poll taken in January 1941, Americans were asked, "If you were asked to vote on the question of the United States entering the war against Germany and Italy, how would you vote—to go into the war or to stay out of the war?" 85 percent of Americans surveyed voted to stay out. During Hitler's war in Europe, the percentage of those wishing to enter the war never rose over 20 percent. In fact, most Americans believed that giving aid to Great Britain offered America the best chance for staying out of the war.[3]

The Midwest had long been a stalwart supporter of isolationism. However, the YWCA and Society for the Cure of Wars, a group made up of concerned women, made a stop in Nebraska in October 1941 and cast doubt on the Midwest's isolationist stance, calling it "over-emphasized." Miss Josephine Schain, leader of the group, stated, "We were agreeably surprised to find that the situation is not as had been reported and that the women of this section are every bit as patriotic as their sisters on the seaboards and in the south."[4] Of course, anecdotal evidence did not a case make for going to war, and women showing their patriotism was far different than being willing to send their menfolk off to war.

Preparing for War

Despite isolationist sentiment, the U.S. government—and Nebraska—had been preparing for war since 1939. From 1939 to 1943, the government added even more agencies to the already bloated consortium created by

FDR's New Deal programs. By 1941, the War Resources Board (1939), the Advisory Commission to the Council of National Defense (1940) and the Office of Production Management had all been created. The Office of Price Administration and Civilian Supply, which would be responsible for rationing once the war began, joined the ranks in August 1941. In the coming years, more agencies would come into being. In fact, the size of the federal government expanded exponentially during the war, dwarfing even its New Deal constraints.

Constructing defense industries and reconverting peacetime manufacturing to a wartime footing became of paramount importance. The government proactively searched for locations, promising not only employment but also a boost to the local economy. In response, Nebraska governor R.L. Cochran ran an ad in the July 7, 1940 issue of the Lincoln Sunday Journal and Star touting Nebraska as the "logical spot" for defense industry. The ad boasted Nebraska's advantages: plenty of water facilities, low electric rates, skilled labor, major railroads, available natural gas and a "spirit of patriotic devotion." The governor's personal note stated:

> I join with the people of Nebraska in this invitation and assure our nation's leaders of the utmost cooperation of all Nebraskans in every respect in carrying out our program of preparedness for national defense. We believe that we have many resources and advantages that should be utilized in this program and we urge that they be employed for the benefit of the nation.[5]

A Lincoln Star editorial of July 10, 1940, echoed the governor's call, insisting that Nebraska's location in the middle of the United States offered it protection from long-range bombers and thus was a perfect place in which to build munitions plants, airplane factories and arms factories. "Failure to take advantage of the isolation of these interior regions," the editorial stated, "will represent a serious blunder but undoubtedly that factor is being given consideration by the responsible individuals and by the newly created national defense council."[6] The governor's plea worked. By December 1940, Nebraska had received a $10 million contract to build an airplane factory in Omaha—what would become the Glenn L. Martin Bomber Plant.

To increase their odds of landing more contracts, as well as having a "medium" through which the national defense council could operate, the new governor of Nebraska, Dwight Griswold, elected in late 1940, created a new advisory defense committee in late January 1941. Griswold said, "It would appear that creation of such a board in Nebraska would acknowledge

Grand Grocery Company storefront, Lincoln, Nebraska. 1942. Library of Congress.

our desire to co-operate with the federal government."[7] By November 1941, every state in the union would have a defense council.[8]

The Nebraska Advisory Defense Committee (NADC), chaired by Griswold, came together quickly and was unanimously approved by the Nebraska Unicameral on February 11, 1941, under L.B. 232.[9] Later that same month, the committee met to plan Nebraska's defense role and to make its case to the U.S. government.[10] It also created a six-point plan for the state:

- Promoting and unifying Nebraskans' patriotism for national defense.
- Mobilizing public support for military, economic and social preparation activities.
- Surveying the economic field, including labor, industry, agriculture, transportation, communication, highways, housing and so on.
- Discouraging and preventing profiteering or unfair advantages of the national defense program by both private and public interests.
- Fostering cooperation in the readjustment of peacetime activities to defense.
- Coordinating lawful efforts to expose, counteract and prevent "Fifth Column" activities, sabotage and other subversive activities while simultaneously preventing hysteria and unwarranted actions against innocent people.[11]

The NADC, with the help of Nebraska businessmen, especially in Lincoln and Omaha, set to work. Two prominent issues revolved around discovering and ultimately securing plants and other projects the federal government wished to place in the area, as well as offering office space for federal workers in Lincoln, Omaha, Grand Island and other Nebraska cities. Senator Norris was also working on their behalf, having "gone to the president directly" to advocate putting a shell-loading plant in Nebraska.[12] By April, the national advisory defense committee's new policy on where to locate defense industries greatly increased Nebraska's chances for landing more defense contracts. With a focus on placing industries in low-population areas away from cities so as not to deplete local labor supply and, instead, to put them in areas that would greatly benefit the economy, where unemployment was higher, meant that several locations in Nebraska were perfect for such defense industries.[13]

Wade Martin, executive vice-chairman of the defense committee, encouraged Nebraska's chambers of commerce to cooperate and make surveys of their communities to support the federal defense program. In a meeting of chamber of commerce secretaries held in Beatrice in May, he asked them to consider two points: "What can we secure from our government in the way of industries, cantonments, air depots, airports, shell loading factories, powder factories, contracts and sub-contracts?" and "What can we offer to our government? It is our feeling that each city should be willing to complete a uniform and comprehensive survey, covering its industrial facilities and community as a whole.…Each city, then, should be willing to accept with grace the chips as they may fall." But Martin also said something that many Nebraskans may have been surprised to hear. Due to the nationwide defense campaign and the country's commitment to such, he noted, "It is now conceded by most thinking people that we are in a state of undeclared war with Germany and the other axis powers."[14]

The NADC also helped communities contend with the housing shortages and zoning issues they might face after defense industries were implemented. Often the committee could offer suggestions, such as how to obtain help from the federal government, on these problems.[15]

In May 1941, Roosevelt created the Office of Civilian Defense (OCD) by Executive Order. This organization's purpose was "to coordinate state and federal measures to protect civilians in a war-related emergency."[16] Through this program, civilians would be taught how to fight fires, supervise blackouts, train air raid wardens and generally be ready to tackle any wartime emergencies that might crop up. It would expand to encourage scrap drives and boost morale and also created the Civil Air Patrol. The program became a huge success. By 1942, as many as 5.6 million Americans and more than 7,000 local councils participated.[17]

Nebraska would be no exception. Wade Martin, a man wearing many defense hats by this point, put on his traveling shoes and made a tour of the state in October 1941 to help organize civilian defense units. In talking to Nebraskans, Martin explained how these groups would be used for fire and police protection, meeting transportation problems and encouraging agricultural production.[18] One month later, the entire country participated in Civilian Defense Week. Already, Americans were saving waste paper, rubber and metal for defense purposes. Martin encouraged Nebraskans to do the same.[19] But even with all of these preparations, Nebraskans still believed that they were "a long way from the war."[20]

Although America was not yet at war, they were already on a war footing. Still, as 1941 drew to a close, many Americans were clinging to the hope that their preparations would be for naught. Unfortunately, on December 7, 1941, that hope vanished.

Robert Osborn, born in Bertrand, Nebraska, was a U.S. Navy radioman stationed at Pearl Harbor at the time of the attack. In a special issue of *Nebraska History* called "What Did You Do in the War?" published in the winter of 1991, Osborn recalled that day:

> ItwasSundaymorning.Itwasatimeofdoingnothing,justrelaxingon theship.IwastopsidetalkingtosomeothershipmateswhentheJapanese camein.Wehadonechiefthererwhotoldmenottogettooexcited.Hesaid, "That'sjustadrill…"Thenaboutfiveortenminuteslater,Isawthe Arizonablowup.Iwasyoung.Iwasn'tscared.Ijustwasamazedmore or less that something like that could happen to us.[21]

The mood in Nebraska, as it did throughout the country, quickly changed from apprehension to anger and vengeance. President Roosevelt moved swiftly, asking Congress for a declaration of war against Japan on December 8, 1941. He met little resistance. Even erstwhile isolationist Senator Norris agreed with the president. "Why of course I'll vote for a declaration of war if one is submitted," Norris said. "I don't see how anyone with a spark of patriotism could do otherwise."[22] Only Jeannette Rankin, a representative from Montana, voted against it. On December 11, 1941, Germany, as an ally of Japan, declared war on America, and America returned the favor, declaring war on Germany only hours later.

The war that America had hoped to avoid was here. Throughout the country, men rushed to enlist. In Lincoln, the U.S. Army and Navy recruiting offices were overrun with men from around the area eager to enlist, and both offices moved to a twenty-four-hour opening period to accommodate the numbers.[23] Shock gripped the University of Nebraska campus in Lincoln. On the Monday following the attacks, classes turned to discussing the war instead of their subjects. Assignments weren't turned in, but it didn't matter as students grappled with the reality of being at war. The Daily Nebraskan, the campus newspaper, reported, "The student body is low. You could sense it 11:30 yesterday morning when groups throughout campus gathered around radios to hear the president address congress."[24]

Following the attack, the editors of the Lincoln Star had sharp words for the isolationists, reflecting the anger and disgust prevalent throughout the nation. "Colonel Lindbergh, Senator Nye, Senator Wheeler, and their lesser lights, by the hundreds, traveling over this country, sowing the seeds of disunion, suspicion, and distrust, have come to the end of their rope. They stand rebuked—rebuked by a sinister, cowardly dastardly attack by a nation without honor or integrity—an attack made even while that nation was professing to desire peace." But the editors also delivered strong words of patriotism and encouragement for Nebraskans. "We go into this war with the most pure ideals that could send any great people into armed conflict. We go into this war to fight to sustain a faith in civilization."[25]

Thanks to its early preparation, the NADC had only to continue with its planning. On December 11, the Lincoln Star reported that twelve regional defense boards had been selected (the defense board for Lincoln and Omaha had already been established), effectively covering the entire state of Nebraska. These committees were responsible for "aiding with county defense unit formation" and urged Nebraskans to wait for the guidance of these committees instead of forming home guard units themselves.[26] Even though the prospect of Nebraska being attacked was incredibly remote, precautions were necessary. A feature in the December 14 issue of the Lincoln Star laid out the program. There were thirteen regional committees, ninety-three county committees and seventeen city committees. Each of these three units would operate through subcommittees. These subcommittees would focus on five areas:

- public relations and finance committee
- civil protection committee
- health, welfare and consumer interest committee
- housing, power, transportation and communications
- agriculture, industry and labor relations[27]

Downtown Lincoln, Nebraska. Circa 1940s. Wikimedia Commons.

Before Pearl Harbor, Nebraskans only half-heartedly volunteered for the civilian defense service, and only about 600 Nebraskans served. After Pearl Harbor, the number went up dramatically, with 4,600 Nebraskans volunteering by January 17, 1942,[28] after a call went out from the Seventh Civilian Defense Region chair, Joseph D. Scholtz. "We need every one of you," Scholtz said. "We need to work as we have never worked before, united, the rich and the poor, the exalted and the humble, in a supreme effort behind the man, behind the gun."[29]

Under the umbrella of the NADC, other committees sprang up, including the State Salvage Committee, the State Nutrition Committee and Public Health Education. These committees were highly visible during the war years, communicating with the public through newspaper articles, meetings, radio broadcasts and pamphlets. Each week, the Nebraska Advisory Defense committee broadcast shows on different topics. For example, during one week in July 1942, the radio station KFAB broadcast shows on health and wellness through food, the scrap campaign and the Nebraska State Guard.[30]

Thanks to the foresight of Nebraska's government, the state was prepared for war. But the challenges were just beginning. In the next four years, Nebraskans would be continually tested in a variety of ways, and each time, they would rise to meet those challenges, sometimes successfully and sometimes not.

RATIONING

During World War I, America did not endure the constraints of rationing. The Great Depression, however, had already taught many Americans how to tighten their belts. Thus, when the rationing program began in December 1941, a few days after the attack on Pearl Harbor, most Americans understood its importance in winning the war. For the next four years, the nation would find unique and inventive ways to get along with less.

The Office of Price Administration's responsibility was to "stabilize prices and rents by setting maximum prices for commodities, except on agricultural products, and maximum rents in defense areas to prevent gouging and inflation." It also established and administered the rationing system and created an extensive public awareness campaign through radio broadcasts, window displays and other media.[31]

Every American man, woman and child received a ration book. Over the war's duration, several books were issued, and the system became rather complicated. Ads and articles appeared in newspapers and magazines to help Americans figure out the process. Every state had its own Office of Price Administration, which implemented the federal regulations. County war price and rationing boards would then register citizens, distribute ration books and administer the program.[32]

It was a massive undertaking. The OPA employed about 60,000 people and relied on more than 195,000 volunteers.[33] Although there were glitches, problems with counterfeit ration books and stamps and an ever-present black market, the rationing system worked relatively well for the duration of the war.

RUBBER AND GAS RATIONING

Since Japan conquered the United States' biggest rubber suppliers, Malaya and the Dutch East Indies, in 1941, tires became one of the first items to be rationed by the U.S. Office of Price Administration. The ration went into effect on December 11, 1941. In Nebraska, tire dealers throughout the state were ordered to submit inventories of their tires and tubes to the NADC. To get a new tire, a Nebraskan had to fill out an application, have his or her old tire inspected and then take the affidavit to the county rationing board for approval. He or she was not allowed to keep the old tire.[34]

In May 1942, gas rationing went into effect on the East Coast, and in October 1942, national speed limits were set at thirty-five miles per hour (except in the case of police, military or emergency vehicles). Both were an attempt to conserve rubber. Some states, like Nebraska, made the lower speed limits voluntary, and Governor Griswold "encouraged" Nebraskans to observe it. "It is for their own best interests," the governor said, "because all tests prove that high rates of speed are very hard on tires and if tires are worn out unnecessarily the cars will go out of use that much sooner."[35]

Gas rationing, however, wasn't voluntary. Even though Griswold strongly objected, pointing to the lack of public transportation and greater traveling distances in the Midwest, Nebraskans still had to submit to the national edict on December 1, 1942.[36] But that didn't mean they were happy about it—in this, they were in solidarity with many other Americans. Across the state, Nebraskans grumbled and complained, and angry letters soon filled Griswold's mailbox. Gas rationing might be all well and good for those living in the cities who had alternative transportation and shorter distances to cover, but in the rural areas of the Midwest, it was a hardship. Several ranching families in the Nebraska Panhandle had to take their children out of school because they didn't have enough gasoline to bring them to school on Monday and then return on Friday to pick them up.[37] Despite public complaints, Nebraska would not be an exception to the rule.

Gas rationing coupons were divided into five classifications, and each classification had its own stamp and a sticker to place on the vehicle's windshield. The rationed amounts and classifications changed during the war, but in general, Class A drivers were considered "nonessential" and were allowed three gallons of gas per week (which was reduced to two on March 22, 1944). Class B vehicles were for business owners and generally restricted to eight gallons. Class C drivers were "essential" drivers—including doctors, clergy, nurses, farm workers, postal carriers and so on—and were unlimited in their ration.

Gas rationing stayed in effect until the war ended in August 1945.

Food Rationing

The first food to be rationed was also the sweetest: sugar. As the Philippines was one of America's largest sugar producers, the Japanese push through the Pacific caused many in America to start hoarding sugar even before the attack on Pearl Harbor. Nine hours after the assault, the Japanese bombed the Philippines. The hoarding only increased. Many economists believed that the massive increase—a 1.2-million-ton increase—of sugar purchased by industrial "sweet-makers" provided strong evidence of hoarding. If the nation, the American military and America's allies wanted sugar for the duration, rationing would be not only prudent but also necessary.[38]

The OPA set out guidelines in February 1942 that made it very clear that hoarders would be punished for their actions. One person per family was required to register, and they had to testify as to how much sugar was currently in their household. One risked a severe fine of $10,000 or ten years imprisonment for lying about their current sugar supply. Those who had more than two pounds of sugar per person were considered "hoarders," had stamps removed from their rationing book and wouldn't receive more until they used up what they'd stockpiled. The government called on public teachers to "personally supervise" ration book distribution, consumer registration and stamp removal of those who had too much sugar. People had to register for their ration books at schools throughout Nebraska. OPA administrator Leon Henderson called it "absolutely necessary" for people to reduce their sugar consumption by one-third.[39]

The sugar ration went into effect in May 1942. Each stamp was good for one pound of sugar for two weeks. In June 1942, one could buy two pounds of sugar with one stamp for a four-week period.[40] It didn't take long for people to devise sugarless or low-sugar recipes for cakes, cookies and other dishes. New recipes appeared in women's magazines, newspaper lifestyle sections and in advertisements from such companies as Betty Crocker, Swan's Down Cake Flour, Spry Vegetable Shortening, Gold Medal Enriched Flour and numerous others.

In April 1942, a full-page article in the Lincoln Sunday Journal and Star promoted the use of alternative sugars, including maple sugar and maple syrup, beet sugar, honey and even sorghum. As in most persuasive articles of the day, the article stressed the importance of doing without so that the armed forces could be in fighting shape to defeat the enemy: "Our guns will bark louder, our boys will fight better because we are buying sugar by the coupon book rather than the sack."[41]

While most Nebraskans accepted sugar rationing without too much fuss, meat rationing was another matter. Meat shortages emerged not long after the war began. But in a state where cattle outnumbered people, limiting beef consumption was particularly grating.

This propaganda poster from the U.S. Office of Price Administration showed Americans how rationing secured fairness in the market. U.S. National Archives, Office for Emergency Management, Office of War Information, Domestic Operations Branch, Bureau of Special Service.

Many meatpackers preferred to sell to the military and the government-sponsored Lend-Lease program instead of to average citizens simply because they could make more money. In response, in early 1942, the government urged Americans to voluntarily limit their meat consumption. But as Douglas Hurt wrote, "By October 1942, the meat supply for civilians had declined by 20 percent. Meatpackers urged grocers to manage their meat supplies so that workers who shopped late in the day would have something to purchase."[42] By January 1943, things hadn't improved, and a black market sprang up. Small towns throughout Nebraska were not immune to such self-indulgence, especially considering it was incredibly easy for farmers and ranchers to sell their meat to neighbors or local grocers who then could turn around and sell it for whatever price they deemed fit. The OPA's price-control program and number of cattle allocated for slaughter in each area tried to stem the tide, but in many respects, it made it worse. By the spring of 1943, ranchers, consumers and meatpackers were fed up.

Clearly, something had to be done. The U.S. Department of Agriculture used a particularly potent combination of fear and education to show Americans that buying black market meat was not only unpatriotic but also hazardous to their health. Black market meat was not inspected by the USDA, which meant neither the animals' health at the time of their slaughter nor the processing and packaging process could be guaranteed. Editorials, ads and newspaper stories pushed this narrative. But they also stressed the deeply troubling effect of the black market on the war effort. It simply wasn't American to buy from the black market. One ad from the American Meat Institute featured a pledge consumers could make to stop the black market in its tracks:

> I will have no part in the black market.
>
> I will not encourage it by demanding meats that are not legitimately available.
>
> I will not stoop to paying illegal prices to keep my Black Market dealer in business or to encourage any honest dealer to enter it.
>
> I will repudiate any person who thinks it is smart or shrewd to obtain Black Market meat.
>
> I will add all the force of my conviction and influence to that of millions of other honest, patriotic Americans to stamp out the evil of the Black Market.
>
> I will have no part of the Black Market—and neither shall you![43]

Unfortunately, these types of pledges did not stop consumers from finding meat where they could, and the meat black market continued for the remainder of the war. Where it could, the OPA prosecuted retailers that participated in the black market, but the system wasn't foolproof.

In Nebraska, cattle rustling was also a concern. But in 1943, officials said it wasn't nearly as big of an issue as people believed. Thanks to the vigilance of the brand committee's special investigators, it had largely been curtailed. Remarkably, most of the cattle rustling incidents occurred in the eastern portion of the state instead of the western counties, which had far larger cattle herds.[44] Meat rationing ended in November 1945.

Throughout the war, other goods were rationed, including silk, coffee, nylons, shoes, typewriters, cheese and more. The War Production Board even restricted the amount of fabric that designers could use in their clothes.[45] But the rationing hardships were miniscule compared to the issues felt in other countries during the war. The government encouraged victory gardens, canning goods and more utilitarian designs in clothing, and Americans responded with ingenious ways to make do with what they had. Americans—and Nebraskans—were usually willing to do their part to help the war effort with minimal complaint.

One Nebraska man, however, wasn't troubled by the regulations. This Lincoln resident noted:

Allthesegovernmentrestrictionsdon'tbothermemuch.Ihaven'tacar, sotiresandgasolinearenoworry.Iwalktoworksotransportationisno problem.Ihavediabetessosugarisnohardship—Ican'teatthestuff. BecauseIhavediabetesthearmywon'ttakeme,andIcanforgetaboutthe draft.Myroomhasbeencoldduringtheentirefall,sowhyworryabout fuelrationingmakingitanycolder.Andtotopitoff...Ineverdidcarefor coffee anyhow.[46]

Chapter 2

NEBRASKA'S ARMY AIRFIELDS

rior to America's involvement in World War II, the United States
government started to expand militarily in fits and starts. In
1927, Congress approved money to increase bases and personnel;
unfortunately, when the Great Depression hit, military funding took a dive.
It took the threat of war in Europe with the Munich Crisis in 1938 to spur
the government into action, and up until America's entry into the war in
1941, the military increased its presence throughout the country with new
air bases and aircraft production. It particularly focused on the interior
region of the United States between the Rocky Mountains in the West and
the Appalachian Mountains in the East. Called the "Citadel of Defense"
in a 1940 report by President Roosevelt's Advisory Commission to the
Council of National Defense, Nebraska became one of the primary survey
targets and proved to be a perfect fit.[47] The requirements for army airfields
were, as Robert Hurst wrote, "level terrain free of natural and man-made
obstructions; a mild climate with an abundance of clear weather flying days;
rural sites to reduce the cost of real estate; reliable public utilities, including
ample electricity, water, and natural gas; access to surface transportation
routes such as paved highways and major railroads; and a large labor pool
for constructing and maintaining the air fields."[48]

Nebraska fit those requirements perfectly, and in early 1942, the
U.S. Army Air Corps announced that eleven army airfields were to be
constructed (the base at Fort Crook already existed) throughout the state:
Ainsworth, Alliance, Bruning, Fairmont, Grand Island, Harvard, Kearney,

Lincoln, McCook, Scottsbluff and Scribner. All the air bases had one thing in common: training men to fight in the air war overseas. These airfields brought changes to small and big towns alike, altering the landscape in more ways than one. Bases functioned as small communities with hospital facilities, barracks, fire stations, chapels and warehouses. Some were smaller than others, but all relied heavily on local towns.

In the July 4, 1943 issue of the Omaha World-Herald, Lieutenant Howard J. Otis had the opportunity to report on the newly constructed airfields in Nebraska:

> It is amazing and exciting to see bombers over the air in Nebraska. It is more amazing to find great expanses of what were farms and beet fields and cattle ranges, converted into tremendous army air bases. Huge air bases, with miles of concrete runways, all permanent installations, with hundreds of the latest planes sitting before hangars, refueling, being tuned up, made ready to fly.[49]

It was, indeed, quite an accomplishment in such a short period of time. The bases varied in size but followed the same standard plans and layouts to conserve material and make the structures last for the duration of the war. To avoid using steel, a critical component of the war effort, the U.S. Army Corps of Engineers used wood, concrete, brick, gypsum board and cement asbestos. Airfields were usually operational within ninety days of construction, a rather remarkable achievement.[50]

Not all bases operated equally. Technical training schools educated bombardiers, pilots, gunners, navigators and mechanics at some bases, while others had more specific training needs. For example, the Alliance airfield had a paratrooper school and trained combat engineers.[51]

Thousands of troops soon descended on Nebraska, swelling the local populations and often creating housing shortages and high rents. But the bases also offered numerous jobs for civilians, boosted the economy and provided new opportunities for women and minorities. In some locations, however, it also created racial tensions, as will be explored in more depth later.

Many bases held competitive sporting events with one another, including baseball and basketball games, and army personnel interacted with civilians in nearby communities at open houses, USO dances, reenactments and parades. The Lincoln Air Base had its own section in the Lincoln newspaper that detailed its activities. During the harvest of 1943, several troops from the McCook airfield even helped farmers with the potato harvest due to the labor shortage.[52]

With the influx of military men, other problems arose. Public health issues, particularly venereal disease and excess drinking, became a concern. The U.S. Public Health Services remembered all too well how venereal diseases had skyrocketed during World War I, thereby reducing the military's effectiveness; it wasn't about to let it happen again. But by 1941, there was already cause for concern. A large number of draft registrants in Oklahoma City tested positive for syphilis, higher than the average around the country. In fact, a great many Great Plains states had a high rate of venereal disease caused by prostitution, extramarital affairs and loosened sexual mores. Nebraska's venereal disease rate remained relatively low, although there were pockets around the state, mostly close to military bases, where it was a problem.[53]

Overall, the airfields created an economic boom to Nebraska towns and offered increased chances to contribute to the war effort through USO groups, war bond rallies and civilian and military gatherings. Nebraskans felt connected to the war and believed they were making a difference.

Although details of some airfields are plentiful, others are not. The majority of the information was found through newspapers and the official U.S. Air Force historical records on microfiche, housed at the History Nebraska archives (formerly known as the Nebraska State Historical Society). It is impossible to tell the complete story of each airfield within this volume, as each could easily have its own book.

Please note that there were several air crashes throughout Nebraska during World War II. Some have been profiled, but not all, in this chapter. For a comprehensive overview of these crashes, please read the excellent work Nebraska's Fatal Air Crashes of World War II by Jerry Penry.

AINSWORTH ARMY AIRFIELD

Ainsworth, a small farming community in Brown County located in north-central Nebraska, became a perfect candidate for an army airfield. A spot was chosen seven miles west of town on a "level piece of prairie land," according to the U.S. Army Corps of Engineers. It served as a satellite base for Rapid City, South Dakota, and was a complete Operational Training Unit Station for the 2nd Air Force. Construction began on the base on September 4, 1942. Three concrete runways and two concrete taxiways were built, along with a control tower, a hangar and a gasoline fueling system.

Sixty-four buildings—which included mess halls, barracks, a dispensary, a post exchange, a warehouse, repair and machine shops, Norden bombsight vaults, a post office, a hospital, office buildings and more—made up the base with room for about six hundred officers and enlisted men. Housing for the soldiers was completed within sixty days, and the base was opened on November 30, 1942.[54]

According to History Nebraska, "The base's primary mission was to provide proficiency training for P-39 and P-47 pilots of the 364th and 53rd fighter squadrons, and for B-17 crews of the 540th and 543rd bombardment squadrons before deployment to the European Theater of Operations."[55]

Around December 10, 1942, about 500 airmen arrived at the base under the command of Major Ralph R. Hawkins. They reached out to the mayor of Ainsworth and several community organizations to discuss the relationship between the citizens and the military. "They have made most favorable impressions," an article in the Ainsworth Star-Journal reported, "and the citizens have made an effort to cooperate to the fullest extent."[56] The people of Ainsworth had been preparing for their arrival and had already organized a military service organization for the airmen in November. They took their mission seriously. "There is a big job ahead for all of us. We must welcome those boys and see that they are properly entertained."[57] It didn't take them long to display their hospitality. The first servicemen's dance was held on December 19 at city hall. Nearly 100 servicemen attended, along with about 125 girls. "This will undoubtedly mark the only dance in which the girls will outnumber the invited guests." A new group of girls over the age of sixteen from Ainsworth, Valentine and other local communities called the "Ainsworth Suzettes" formed. Under the watchful eye of their hostesses, these girls had to abide by the simple rules of similar USO groups in Lincoln (please see the information about the Lincolnettes group in chapter 8) in order to provide dance partners for the Ainsworth servicemen.[58]

Beginning with the December 24, 1942 issue of the Ainsworth Star-Journal, a regular feature appeared called simply "News from the Air Base." In this column, military personnel kept the townspeople apprised of the activities at the base and informed them of some of the more technical aspects of their jobs. In the first column, it described the air base's daily activities and profiled some of the officers. It also praised the people of Ainsworth for the donations received for the base's day room, including ping pong tables, divans, magazines, games and more. "It is the one place a fellow can go to relax, read, listen to a favorite radio program, or write a letter."[59] The next column explained the ins and outs of what the combat and ground crews did while training in the B-17s, offered gratitude for the invitations from the "good ladies of the community to eat Christmas dinner with them and their families" and profiled the commanding officer, Major Hawkins. The Ainsworth mayor also praised the townspeople for welcoming the airmen but also reminded them to act with grace and leniency to deal with the crowded housing conditions and other issues that might arise due to the influx of servicemen.[60]

Ainsworth citizens also had to deal with the sound of training exercises twenty-four hours a day, but the "News from the Air Base" column made sure to tell them why this training was so important. "The planes fly night and day, for both phases of training are important in war work….The crews in the planes are learning combat tactics, gunnery and bombing. A flier never ceases to learn, and the more things he learns the more chances he will have of keeping out of trouble."[61]

Besides training for war, the airmen kept busy with other activities. They started a basketball team almost as soon as they arrived in December 1942 called the 2nd Air Force Bluejays. They often played the Ainsworth High School team. By June 1943, a baseball team had been organized (they played the Ainsworth Firemen team), as well as a volleyball team. Church services, USO entertainments, dances and other community activities also kept the airmen entertained. In August 1943, the Victory Book Campaign donated three thousand books to the base library, fiction and nonfiction. That same month, a former member of Tommy Dorsey's band, Private Frank Lombardi, who was stationed at the air base, put on an impromptu piano concert at the USO Hall in town.[62]

In addition to bomber training, the base had a camouflage school. The Engineer Camouflage Aviation Battalion arrived in August 1943, and one of its officers, Captain Saltus, said, "Ainsworth is one of the finest western towns I've ever had the pleasure to visit."[63] Scribner Air Base also had a camouflage school.

Inexplicably, the "News from the Air Base" column ceased publication in the Ainsworth Star-Journal in late 1943, leaving two years of the story of the air base untold. After the war ended, the base closed in December 1945. Today, there are still some buildings standing from the World War II era, and it is now used as the Ainsworth Regional Airport.

ALLIANCE ARMY AIRFIELD

Located in the Nebraska Panhandle on the edge of the Sandhills, the bustling railroad town of Alliance boasted a population of nearly 6,700 people by 1940 and served as a central locale for farmers and ranchers in the region. On April 15, 1942, the secretary of war authorized Alliance as an army airfield. That summer, construction began and "over 5,000 construction workers had swarmed into Alliance, nearly doubling the size of the town." These construction workers included Sioux Indians from the Pine Ridge and Rosebud Reservations, African Americans from Kansas City and Wichita and Mexicans from the Southwest.[64] By the time they finished, they'd built 775 buildings, 35,503 feet of runway and 12,332 feet of taxiways.[65]

Activated in August 1942, Major J.C. Calvert, an aviation veteran from World War I, took command of the base.[66] It served as an Air Support Transport Glider Station (C-47 Waco CG-4A gliders were pulled aloft by Douglas C-47 Skytrains) for the First Troop Carrier Command, 434th Carrier Group. The 411th Army Air Forces Base Unit, as part of the Air Technical Service Command, commanded the support elements. Originally, it was to be a training facility for paratroopers and air commandos. But the base's mission changed, and it "became a field for the combined training of Troop Carrier and Airborne Forces; pilots, co-pilots, glider pilots, airborne engineers for the Troop Carrier Command, paratroopers, airborne infantry, and artillery for the Airborne Forces."[67] The 411th Base Headquarters Squadron, 403rd and 434th Troop Carrier Groups, 326th Glider Infantry, 507th Parachute Infantry and 878th Airborne Engineers were stationed here. In May 1943, fifteen black enlisted men from Baer Air Field in Indiana arrived as part of the 443rd Aviation Squadron.[68]

In April 1944, the base was reorganized, re-designated as the 805th Air Base Unit and became a Replacement Training Unit.[69] By September 1944, the 2nd Air Force had assumed jurisdiction over the base for the training of B-29 Superfortress crews. The 1st Troop Carrier Command returned in 1945 to train for the proposed invasion of Japan. This was, of course, cut short after the dropping of the atomic bombs.[70]

From the beginning, a housing and civilian personnel shortage plagued Alliance and the base. Trailer camps and additional housing construction partially solved the problem, but the personnel shortage was harder to combat. Area residents didn't want to work for the air base due to the low wage. Therefore, the army had to recruit workers from around the country. Men and women from Oklahoma, New York, California, Michigan and other states ended up fulfilling the civilian positions, which included typists, aircraft mechanics, stenographers, dental technicians, radio mechanics and more.[71]

Before the first prisoner of war arrived to occupy the new POW camp at Fort Robinson in 1943, a detachment of seventy-five men from the Alliance Air Base arrived in July 1943 and occupied the camp. They had to repair and reclaim gliders that had been damaged during maneuvers. Although the men felt that the living conditions were "irritating" (receiving mail was one gripe, although they solved the problem by having a flight officer from Alliance fly the mail directly to Fort Robinson), they accomplished their mission and stayed through August 1943 before returning to Alliance.[72]

The base's official dedication occurred on August 22, 1943, and more than sixty thousand people gathered for the festivities, including Nebraska governor Dwight Griswold. To mark the occasion, the troops reenacted the invasion of Sicily (which had occurred from July 9 to August 17, 1943) and ably demonstrated the reasons for airborne troops' indispensable participation in the operation. Burt James, a reporter for the Lincoln Star, wrote, "Sitting under a hot, cloudless sky observers were given a real view of war conditions as paratroopers tumbled out of planes 500 to 600 feet from the ground and gliders spilled men and equipment as they came in behind bombers and pursuit ships." Other activities included a chemical warfare demonstration, stunt flying in gliders, a military retreat and the induction of the base's Women's Army Air Corps (WAACs) group.[73]

However, perhaps the most astonishing event of the day featured the mascot of the 507th: a German shepherd named Geronimo. Owned by Private Kenneth Williams of the 507th Parachute Infantry, Geronimo jumped along with his fellow paratroopers that day, gliding gently to the earth carrying first aid supplies. LIFE magazine even featured the dog and his performance in its September 13, 1943 issue.[74] Geronimo participated in other jumping spectacles for audiences in Omaha and Denver but was never sent overseas.

The relationship between the base and the city of Alliance had its ups and downs. A report from the Legal and Claims division of the base lamented the lack of morale-building from the community. "The civilian population did little or nothing to increase recreational and entertainment facilities with the influx of soldiers," it stated. It recommended recreational facilities be increased at the base so that it would be "unnecessary for military personnel to seek entertainment in the city of Alliance." The report also suggested that "[c]ivilians should be taught tactfully and properly the value

Offices at the Alliance Army Air Base.
Knight Museum and Sandhills Center.

of directing military personnel in a better fashion" and also encouraged improved liaison between the city and the base to help control prices and transportation efforts.[75]

At its core, the relationship between the base and the city of Alliance could perhaps best be described as strained. Another entry in the Legal and Claims division provided still more proof. "From my experience, the relationship of the citizens of Alliance to Air Base personnel has been and still is extremely bad," the author stated (his name is not attached to the report). He then went on to cite personal experiences as well as conversations with civilian and military personnel to support his comment.[76] However, the public relations office report stated that the relationship between the citizens of Alliance and the air base had been "amicably maintained."[77] But in a historical report written in March 1944, interviews with two base officers provide a blistering commentary on military relations with the town. Second Lieutenant James. J. Rochn listed several examples of how Alliance merchants and private citizens took advantage of the military personnel, jacking up the prices for rent and goods. He compared the police force to a "comic strip" and lamented the appalling way they treated "Indian squaws," something Rochn personally witnessed numerous times. "In summary," Rochn wrote, "this observer feels that the attitude of the citizenry is entirely motivated by greed to make the most out of 'easy pickins' while the time is ripe. They know someday that the war will end and that they won't have so much money flooding the town."[78] In another interview, a captain at the air base stated, "The city did not seem to realize that they would have to give more than they would receive. They did little to provide for new personnel, civilian or military."[79]

But there were also Alliance civilians dedicated to the base's success. "A few notable individuals made a great effort to better the conditions and raise the soldiers' morale," wrote Daw in the historical report.[80] Articles in the Alliance Times-Herald report that because the USO was slow in setting up a USO spot for the airmen, numerous Alliance citizens in November 1942 wanted to give the soldiers the use of the city auditorium.[81] In that same month, Alliance women chaperoned local girls (sixteen and older)

Top: Airmen pose for a photo at the Alliance Army Air Base. Knight Museum and Sandhills Center.

Middle: Airmen on parade for the local townspeople. Alliance Army Air Base. Knight Museum and Sandhills Center.

Bottom: Airmen, possibly from the 507th Parachute Infantry Regiment, march in formation. Alliance Army Air Base. Knight Museum and Sandhills Center.

Top: The 507th Parachute Infantry glides to the earth during its mock battle of Sicily at the Alliance Army Air Base on August 22, 1943. Knight Museum and Sandhills Center.

Middle: Geronimo poses after his successful jump during the mock battle of Sicily at the Alliance Army Air Base on August 22, 1943. Knight Museum and Sandhills Center.

Bottom: Private Kenneth Williams of the 507th Parachute Infantry poses with his dog, Geronimo, after his successful jump on August 22, 1943. Knight Museum and Sandhills Center.

Geronimo and his owner, Private Kenneth Williams of the 507th Parachute Infantry, prepare to jump. No known copyright restrictions.

to dances at the air base because there was not yet a USO set up in the town. Army troop trucks were used to transport the girls to and from the dance.[82] The base's public relations officer regularly sent out press releases and, in May 1944, even arranged to have a sixteen-page special insert in the Alliance Times-Herald detailing the history of the base up until that point.[83] Alliance citizens also visited ailing soldiers at the base during the Christmas season and even donated coat hangers twice, once in October 1942 and again in January 1943, along with books and games.[84] A USO Center was temporarily located at 212 Box Butte Avenue, and a new one was later constructed at the site of the old city hall.

To continue to improve relations between the community and the soldiers, and also to increase morale, the Special Service Branch, responsible for the soldiers' entertainment, set up a program called Home Hospitality. Each week, citizens from Alliance and the surrounding area invited soldiers to their homes. No fewer than fifty soldiers participated every week. For Thanksgiving Day in 1943, more than two hundred men had dinner with local families.[85]

When asked "In your opinion, what has been the attitude of the people of Alliance toward the military personnel?" Alliance citizen Clarence Hoper responded, "We were anxious to get an army camp here. The soldiers were gladly received, many of them were invited into our homes and some of them have become real friends. It is true that a city of 6,000 would have some problems."[86]

More interviews seem to come to the general consensus that relations between the city and the base were congenial in the first months of the base's existence but soured as more soldiers arrived. Greed, a term used in several interviews, became a factor, leading to high rents for unsatisfactory and downright terrible housing options and higher prices. As Captain William H. Hutchinson stated, "The principle trouble arose because Alliance wanted and obtained an Air Base, but did not anticipate the problems it would create."[87] This could undoubtedly be stated for the majority of air bases located near small towns during the war, as it strained local economies to provide adequate housing, goods and services.

Of course, some soldiers' disreputable behavior in Alliance made things worse. In one incident, an enlisted soldier of the 507th Parachute Infantry Regiment followed a woman home and chased her into her kitchen. Her husband commenced to give him a "sound beating" before turning him over to the military authorities. In another incident, a dead cow, shot three times, was found on the Peterson Brothers Ranch, and officials found that the death was "deliberate and malicious."[88] Cases of public drunkenness and fighting also occurred, which certainly didn't endear the citizens to the military personnel.

Morale continued to be an issue throughout the life of the Alliance Army Air Base. Content soldiers meant fewer problems, less venereal disease and less friction with civilians. The Special Services Branch provided a number of activities for those stationed at the air base. Their post theater enjoyed robust attendance. Here they showed training and orientation films, newsreels, lectures and Hollywood movies. In the gymnasium, soldiers enjoyed sports of all kinds, including baseball, softball, basketball, ping pong, ice skating and volleyball. In addition, world heavyweight boxing champion Joe Louis held an exhibition match here as part of his celebrity tour during World War II. (Louis voluntarily enlisted in the U.S. Army in January 1942.) The library boasted more than five thousand books, and the dance orchestra performed more than three hundred times between March 1943 and March 1944. In addition, the army band played for retreats, reviews and army ceremonies.[89] The base's 103 Club held several activities to help keep up morale. Checkers, ping pong and chess tournaments were popular, as were bingo, variety shows, dances and community song fests. The club also had a letter-writing center, "complete with stationery and ink furnished." The Special Services also hosted seventy-five USO shows between March 1943 and March 1944.[90]

It is important to note, however, that the majority of these recreational activities were limited to white troops. The black soldiers from the 443rd did not have access to a USO club or the 103 Club. This created tension between white and black soldiers, and although some fights broke out, they were not serious. In response, the army and the town collaborated to open a USO club exclusively for black soldiers, as well as a club similar to the 103 Club on the base itself. In addition, one night a week was reserved for black soldiers at the base's bowling alley.[91]

Beginning in July 1943, a section of WAACS (later WACS) served at the Alliance base. The women came from Massachusetts, Georgia and Iowa. They were assigned to work in nearly every office on the base, and due to their "diligence and attention to duty," they "gradually overcame the women's-place-is-in-the-home prejudice, a real obstacle to their usefulness in the army."[92] In a history of the air base written by Sergeant Joseph W. Daw, the historian agreed. "The caliber of the work being done by the WAC's has proved that the women are capable, well disciplined, and anxious to serve."[93] The WACS sponsored a glee club

Left to right: Staff Sergeant M.W. Slidinger, Lieutenant Jeffrey Roche, Major Albert S. Dubbin, Corporal Joe R. Carlton, Phyllis Grove and Corporal E.R. McAllen. Alliance Army Air Base. Knight Museum and Sandhills Center.

for male and female officers, and the group performed at a candlelight service a few days before Christmas. In addition, they were involved in several training programs on the base, including military customs and discipline, camouflage, inspection, defense against chemical attack and more. However, none of these training programs involved the use of training for firearms.[94]

Unfortunately, several Alliance airmen perished in training accidents. On May 28, 1943, Flight Officer Charles B. Edwards took off from the base in his L-3B Grasshopper aircraft. He arrived at the municipal airport and began practicing landings and takeoffs. During one practice run, Edwards lost control of the plane and hit the ground at a steep angle. The impact was strong enough to severely injure Edwards, and he later died from his injuries. The investigation concluded that Edwards had used "poor technique" and that there was nothing mechanically wrong with the plane.[95]

A second fatal crash occurred only two months later near Hemingford. Six planes took off from the Alliance base for a scheduled four-hour practice formation. The C-53 plane piloted by Second Lieutenant Theodore K. Chapman came down on top of Second Lieutenant John R. Hunter's C-47 plane. Chapman's motor caught fire, and both planes lost control. They spiraled toward the ground, where Chapman's C-53 became completely engulfed in flames. The investigation determined the cause of the crash as "pilot error due to lack of experience." Unfortunately, both planes each had three other passengers: all eight perished.[96]

In September 1943, two Alliance airmen, pilot Second Lieutenant William Cardia and copilot Second Lieutenant Robert G. Bartels, crashed their C-53D "Skytrooper" plane. The two died instantly at the crash site six miles south of Alliance. The cause of the crash was never determined.[97]

After the war ended, the air base was declared surplus in 1945. Several of the buildings were sold off, but the status of the airfield remained in limbo for years. In 1953, the U.S. government sold part of the base and the remaining buildings to the City of Alliance. It became the Alliance Municipal Airport, which is still in operation today.[98]

BRUNING ARMY AIRFIELD

Unlike some of the other bases across Nebraska, files and information on the Bruning Air Field, located in Thayer County, Nebraska, are not as plentiful. Official records from the United States Air Force are minimal, making it difficult to tell the base's complete story. However, local newspapers, the Bruning Banner and the Hebron Journal, kept residents apprised of much of the base's activities, and the book Those Who Flew includes stories about the satellite air base and memories of those connected with it.

Today, fewer than 300 people make up the village of Bruning. In 1942, when construction began on the air base about six miles east of the village, the population was even smaller: a little more than 230 residents. Other small towns nearby, like Fairbury and Hebron, were larger but still lacked the entertainment many soldiers looked for while on weekend passes. Still, that wasn't necessarily a bad thing. In a 1998 letter to Virginia Priefert, the president of the Thayer County Historical Society, Lieutenant Colonel Pat Gentry wrote that being stationed in a place lacking amenities and distractions was "a blessing in disguise":

> Lookingbacknowfrommy80yearoldvantagepoint,Bruningservedit's [sic]purposeverywell.Wehadonlyafewshortweekstodoacriticaljob. Wehadtotaketenstrangersfromeachcrew,putthemtogetherasacohesive unit,givethemthebasicrudimentarytrainingasacombatteam,and convincethemthatwecouldsurviveatleastlongenoughtoreachthecombat zone.HadBruningbeenotherthanaquiet,ruralstation,theproblems would have been more severe.[99]

As had happened at other base locations and war projects across Nebraska, in September 1942, local farmers were ordered to vacate their land within ten days and were paid nowhere near what their land was worth. Construction began on the 1,720-acre base, and an influx of carpenters and other workers flooded the area, creating, as it had in other small towns, a housing shortage. The government responded by authorizing housing projects in Hebron, Bruning and Ohiowa in May and June 1943.[100]

The base was dedicated on August 28, 1943. It began as a B-24 training base, and the 456th, 449th and 487th Heavy Bombardment Groups were stationed here. This changed in 1944 when P-47 pilots from the 23rd Fighter Squadron and the 507th and 508th Fighter Groups trained at the base.

The Special Service Department history report from October 1943 praised the high morale of the base and the low number of violations, crediting the Special Services for its work in this area. Because the base's remote location made entertaining the troops difficult, the Special Services worked hard to provide entertainment. They immediately improvised a movie theater in one of the small supply buildings and started screening 16mm Hollywood films three times a week and then increased it six times a week with two showings each night. Admission was ten cents per showing, and even though it cost the Special Services about twenty-five dollars to rent the films from companies in New York and Chicago, the theater made a small profit. Word of its success spread, and other air bases began to ask the Bruning Special Services Department for advice on how to duplicate it. The department was happy to offer its advice.[101]

Traveling USO shows performed about twice a month, and the base also put out a newspaper called the Baafler. In July 1943, the chapel opened. According to an article in the Nebraska State Journal, army chapels shared a similar design that could be easily changed to suit each air base. The Bruning base chapel was described as "a distinctive oblong shaped wooden building, with a high-arched roof and a tall spire that is a landmark on the field. Its amber-stained windows provide a mellow sunlight, in keeping with the purpose of the building. Large wooden trusses, from which rustic wooden light fixtures are suspended, lend a feeling of solemn dignity to the interior."[102]

With the help of the Bruning and Hebron communities, plus several other neighboring villages, the base established day rooms and a service club. Donations of furniture, games, rugs, books and more came from around the area.[103] In addition, servicemen stayed busy with basketball and baseball games with neighboring air base teams.

Some airmen based at Bruning also lost their lives due to plane crashes. In July 1944 alone, eleven men were killed. On July 5, 1944, Second Lieutenant William D. Hearn crashed his P-47D "Thunderbolt" plane during a practice run seven miles north of the village of Meadow Grove and was killed instantly.[104] Only two days later, another fatal crash occurred, this time on the Bruning field itself. Flight Officer Don M. Peterson was approaching the Bruning runway with his P-47G "Thunderbolt" when he turned too slow and caused the plane to stall. He crashed, and the plane cartwheeled and then exploded. Peterson was killed.[105] During a mock conflict training between a formation of B-17F Flying Fortress bombers and P-47D "Thunderbolts" near Daykin, Second Lieutenant Charles "Chuck" F. Jewett, piloting his P-47, collided with one of the B-17s. Jewett's plane dove toward the ground and crashed, killing him instantly. Three men from the B-17—Corporal Leonard J. Rizutti, Corporal Salvador V. Halcón and Second Lieutenant Wallace E. Clements—parachuted to safety. The other crew members were killed. In total, eight men died that day.[106] On July 31, 1944, a P-47D "Thunderbolt," piloted by Second Lieutenant Thomas L. Clark, was flying with four other P-47s during training exercises when Clark lost control and crashed on a farm northwest of Powell. His injuries were massive, and he did not survive.[107]

Another terrible crash involving airmen from the Bruning Army Air Base happened on August 3, 1944. A C-47A "Skytrain" carrying twenty-eight airmen crashed near Naper, Nebraska, close to the border of South Dakota. According to an article in the Lincoln Evening State Journal, "By horse and wagon bodies were brought from the wreckage a distance of two miles to the highway. The wreckage was scattered over an area of about two miles."[108] The airmen included twenty-four P-47 pilots who had just graduated from the 262nd Fighter Pilot Training School at Bruning. The exact cause of the crash was never fully determined, but weather appears to have played a factor. "After one very heavy lightning flash, the noise coming from the engines of the plane immediately stopped," Penry wrote. "A few moments later the plane was seen coming out of the base of the cloud in a very steep dive. During the dive the plane flipped upside down as it continued downward with no apparent attempt at recovery. The plane was still inverted when it struck the ground."[109] A memorial to the lost airmen is located in the Naper Cemetery along Highway 12.

After the war ended, Bruning was declared surplus by the U.S. War Department in November 1945, and Nebraska regained control of it until 1969, when it was reverted to agricultural use once again.

FAIRMONT ARMY AIRFIELD

Located between the small Nebraska towns of Fairmont and Geneva in Fillbury County, the Fairmont Army Airfield served as the final training location for the 451st, 485th, 504th and 16th Heavy Bombardment Groups before they were sent overseas. In addition, the 98th, 467th and 489th Bombardment Groups returning from Europe trained here for possible duty in the Pacific. Construction began in September 1942, and the field originally served as a satellite of the Topeka Army Air Base. Later, in 1943, it came under the command of 2nd Air Force Headquarters in Colorado Springs, Colorado.

Due to the influx of construction workers, a housing shortage emerged in Geneva and Fairmont, much as it had in other locations across the state. The field and buildings were finished within ninety days, however, and included one of the largest hospitals in Nebraska at the time. In addition to barracks and hangars, the base had a movie theater, a service club, a post exchange, a barbershop and a library. About six hundred civilians worked at the base, and more than three thousand airmen served here.[110]

The airfield also had a weekly newsletter to announce events, war bond drives, editorials, sports and news about each bombardment group. Several activities kept the airmen busy. For example, one week's worth of activities included bingo, four dances, a movie and a band novelty program, all sponsored by the service club.[111] Softball, baseball and boxing clubs existed for the airmen to participate in, and they traveled to play other army air force teams in Nebraska.

According to the May 1944 history of the base, morale was very high at Fairmont. The support of the baseball team and large attendance at boxing matches, as well as the "splendid manner" in which the servicemen conducted themselves during training, inspections, retreats and parades, all provided evidence of such.[112]

The airfield also asked local teenagers to help at the base during the summer of 1944, and the program was extremely successful. In addition to providing extra manpower, the program also helped increase good relations between the base and the communities.[113]

Perhaps the most significant event that occurred at the airfield was the arrival of Lieutenant Colonel Paul Tibbets in September 1944, although its significance would not be known to servicemen at the base until after the war. Tibbets picked several crew and their support personnel for the training of what would be the dropping of the atomic bombs on Hiroshima and Nagasaki.[114]

After the war ended, the field was deactivated in 1945. However, today it is still in use as an airfield for crop dusters and civilian pilots. Several buildings remain, including four hangars and the water tower.

GRAND ISLAND ARMY AIRFIELD

It is rather difficult to piece together the story of the Grand Island Air Base. Unfortunately, the official U.S. Army Air Forces records are not available. Nevertheless, the air base, like the Cornhusker Ordnance Plant, had a major effect on the town of Grand Island. The Grand Island Independent newspaper kept its pulse on the activities at the field and provided numerous details of its happenings. A daily column for the airmen simply titled "Air Base News" ran in the paper and included details on USO dances, men on furlough, visitors to the base, sporting event announcements, marriages and births and more. It appears that the soldiers and the citizens of Grand Island enjoyed a good relationship, as airmen often went to people's homes for holiday dinners and other get-togethers.

Located about three miles northeast of Grand Island in Hall County, the base was built on the site of Grand Island's Arrasmith Airport. Construction began in 1942, and it was originally to be used as a satellite field but was expanded to be its own independent base by early 1943. It was difficult to find labor to build the base, but "business and professional men from Grand Island" answered the call and worked night shifts and even on Sundays to finish base construction.[115] By April 1943, the base was officially activated. It was under the command of the 2nd Air Force Headquarters in Colorado Springs, Colorado. Over the course of the field's history, about 3,500 airmen trained here with B-17 and B-29 bombers for service overseas. Bombardment groups includes those from the 6th, 502nd, 449th, 28th and 376th Bombardment Groups.

On the day of the base's public opening ceremony, June 12, 1943, Governor Dwight Griswold and Senator Hugh Butler came to the festivities, which included a public program and a tour of the base for the general public. The previous day, the Grand Island Independent featured several ads from local businesses welcoming the airmen to the city, as well as the employees of the Cornhusker Ordnance Plant. In addition, the paper ran several stories about the air base. The base hospital was an "impressive cluster of snow white buildings" that included X-ray and laboratory rooms in addition to the wards and mess halls.[116] The new chapel was reminiscent of New England churches and provided services for Protestants, Catholics and Jews. The chapel also included a new Hammond organ. The story went on to describe the chapel's beauty:

Within the nave there are thirty-two rustic stained pews, each having a capacity of 384 persons. Each pew is equipped with a kneeler and prayer book rack similar to those used in large churches. To heighten the simple rustic effect, the side walls of the chapel are made of knotty pine wainscoting, above which is celotex planking of various colors extending to the ceiling line and blending into the wainscoting and the four exposed stained walnut trusses. To perfect the harmony in coloring, each side of the nave is decorated with five windows of brown stained cathedral glass of a hammered pattern. The lighting fixtures are also of rustic color being constructed of hardwood of variegated color and hung and ornamented with hammered iron.[117]

The Special Services office at the base was responsible for keeping up the men's morale, believing it would make them better soldiers. "It is the firm belief of the men behind the special services setup that a soldier who is better acquainted with the American way of life through entertainment and who is one amongst his brethren, socially and otherwise, will make a better soldier and citizen."[118] The group was responsible for scheduling theater and USO shows, arranging church services, running the camp newspaper, organizing sports team, offering classes and more.

At the Grand Island base, there was an Officers Club and a recreation center, which included a theater and a gymnasium. The men at the air base also took part in sporting activities, such as softball, baseball, boxing, bowling and basketball. The Base Service Club opened up in June 1943 and held dances on a regular basis. "No finer clubroom of its size can be easily found where good taste and common sense prevails over the choice selection of its properties," read an article in the Grand Island Independent. "Only the finest in leather upholstery and its accessories are used to fill this room. A superb Magnovax radio-phonograph capable of playing 14 continuous records in a beautiful mahogany cabinet exemplifies the taste of a connoisseur."[119]

Of course, the airmen also had a job to do. Preparing bombing crews for overseas missions was of paramount importance at the base, as was maintaining the aircraft. The 424th Sub-Depot, a military organization manned mostly by civilians, was responsible for keeping aircraft in working order at Grand Island.

A group of six WASPs (Women Airforce Service Pilots) also served here and flew B-17s, C-47s, C-45s, UC-78s and L-5s as utility, engineering, administrative, tracking and cargo transport pilots. One of them was Mary H. Gosnell, who would later go on to ferry documents and personnel involved with the atomic bomb.[120]

After the war ended, the base became a Strategic Air Command base (SAC) until October 31, 1946, when it was again returned to the city of Grand Island for use as an airport.

HARVARD ARMY AIRFIELD

Located in Clay County, the Harvard Army Airfield was a few miles northeast of the town of Harvard and served as a satellite base of the Kearney Army Airfield. Construction began in September 1942, and the field was activated in December of that same year. Bombardment groups that trained here included the 447th (B-17s); the 484th (B-24s); and the 505th, 501st, 45th, 376th and 476th (B-29s).

During its time as an airfield, the number of military and civilian personnel fluctuated. Personnel increased in June 1944, and the housing shortage became acute. Because the Hastings Naval Ammunition Depot was located nearby, this affected available off-base housing for military families. Thus, the base turned to the Federal Housing Authority for relief. The proximity of the depot also caused a labor shortage at the base since the depot offered "a much higher wage than can be afforded by the base."[121] By October 1944, the total number of military and civilian personnel was 6,284.[122]

The base enjoyed USO shows and even took a bus of servicemen to Lincoln to watch the 2nd Air Force Superbombers versus "Iowa Seahawk football game" (it is possible the historical officer recorded the wrong name, as they are the Iowa Hawkeyes). Men could also purchase hunting licenses and take trips to Hastings to watch high school football games. In addition, the men enjoyed other theater performances, although the historical officer reported in October 1944 that there was difficulty in keeping patrons in their seats until the performances ended. In what was surely reminiscent of high school days, theater personnel were strategically placed throughout the theater, and when patrons rose early to leave, they were told to sit down. Apparently this plan worked, although why patrons wanted to escape performances early is unknown.[123]

A weekly newsletter, the Harvard Accent, kept the airmen abreast of activities on the base and war news. It also included book and movie reviews, a column by the chaplain, a schedule of USO shows and movies and sports news from the servicemen's sporting teams.

The field was declared surplus property in May 1946. One of the original hangars still stands today.

KEARNEY ARMY AIRFIELD

Thanks to students at the University of Nebraska–Kearney, much has been written about the Kearney Army Airfield, including master's theses and dissertations. UNK's History Department's digital history project on Kearney's history has a wealth of information on the base, including oral histories, photos and scrapbooks.[124] The Buffalo County Historical Society has also written a fine history of the base with details from soldiers and civilians who worked there.

Before the war began, the City of Kearney lobbied to have a military facility. The city built an airport in August 1942 in the hopes of attracting an air base. It worked, but unfortunately, when the U.S. Army inspected the airport, it determined it would be inadequate for heavy bombers. Thus, the new airport had to be rebuilt in accordance with army regulations. Construction began in September 1942, and as had happened with other war projects in Nebraska, about 2,200 acres of nearby farmland were condemned and used for base construction. Paving projects ended in November 1942, and construction ceased on February 1, 1943.[125]

The base started out as a processing unit that consisted of "maintenance checks on the planes and last-minute training and preparation for the crews" before air crews were sent overseas for combat duty. The 100th Army Bombardment Group arrived with its B-17 Flying Fortresses on February 4, 1943, and went through processing before going overseas for service with the 8th Army Air Forces in Europe. Following their departure, the base became a training center for replacements from August through November 1943 and then became a processing center again. Kearney became part of the 7th Heavy Bombardment Processing Headquarters[126]

U.S. Army Air Corps personnel stand in front of a B-17 Flying Fortress. Kearney Army Air Base. March 11, 1944. Buffalo County Historical Society Trails & Rails Museum.

What, exactly, did processing entail? Todd L. Petersen outlined it as follows:

> TheresponsibilitiesoftheSeventhProcessingHQincludedperforming maintenancechecksontheairplanes,primarilyB-17sandB-29s,toinsure [sic]thebestpossibleperformancewhentheydepartedtheUnitedStates. ThemenwhooperatedthesebomberswerealsoprocessedatKearney. Combatcrewprocessingconsistedofissuingthepropergear,checkingtosee thatallinoculationswereuptodate,providinglastminuteinstructions,and havingthemenwritewills.Crewmenwerealsotestedtodetermineifany ofthemwereunfitforcombatduty.Theprocedurestookfromthreetoseven days.WhenthemenleftKearney,theyproceededtoaportofembarkation andthenwentdirectlytoacombatzone.Tensofthousandsofsoldiers wereprocessedatKearney.Formanyitwastheirlastopportunityfora passwhileinthestates,leavingKearneywiththedilemmaofproviding amusement to hordes of restive young men.[127]

Mechanics replace an engine in a B-17. Kearney Army Air Base. Buffalo County Historical Society Trails and Rails Museum.

Six hangars, barracks, warehouses, a post office, a hospital, a recreation hall, a theater, a chapel, a post exchange, mess halls and other buildings composed the base. With the influx of construction workers and, soon, the military and civilian workers, housing became critical. Kearney had a population of just under ten thousand people, and it still could not board everyone. Hotels and boarding rooms quickly filled, and the city council voted to relax the ordnance on trailer parking on private property. Trailers soon appeared nearly everywhere, but housing remained an issue for the duration of the war.[128]

The Kearney Air Base News newspaper (later renamed The Duster) published its first issue on April 9, 1943. On the first page appeared a welcome from the mayor of Kearney, Ivan Mattson, to all the servicemen: "We extend our hand—we give you our recreational facilities, our parks, our churches, our homes, and our sincerest friendship."[129] Indeed, the citizens of Kearney took their responsibility to the base seriously. They formed the Kearney Recreation Committee (later renamed the War Recreation Committee) and quickly raised funds for a new service center. The committee chose the old Safeway building at 2006–9 Center Avenue and remodeled it, opening it for business in January 1943. It was later taken over by the USO. In addition, Kearney women created a Hostess Corps to help with dances, games and daily service center duties. Hostesses had to be at least eighteen years old, have good values and be single, and there were always chaperones at every activity to make sure nothing untoward happened between the soldiers and the hostesses.[130]

However, despite the city's best intentions, problems did develop between the soldiers, local girls and so-called Victory Girls who came from as far away as Oklahoma. Five brothels also popped up in town. The police's laissez-faire attitude to them didn't help. Even though the base had several condom distribution centers, the venereal infection rate soared in 1944, and in February of that same year, the military base implemented a one-month midnight curfew for all military members to help curb infections. But by August 1945, the infection rate had once again gone up, although this time, the surgeon on base decided that the increase was due to "excessive drinking and celebrating brought about by the news of the Japanese surrender."[131]

Another point of contention in Kearney concerned the black troops stationed at the base. Because of segregation, black troops had to have a separate service center. Some Kearney citizens did not want this service center located in their neighborhood and made their concerns known to the city council. Despite the residents' objections, a new service center called the 366 Club for black Americans at 2222 Avenue A opened at the end of March 1943. Because there were no black women in the Hostess Corps in Kearney for dances, the Urban League Club in Lincoln sent three truckloads of black women to help entertain the black servicemen in July 1943.[132] Others came from Omaha. In addition, the War Recreation Board also built a swimming pool for black servicemen.

However, despite some of these issues, the citizens of Kearney and other local communities like Gibbon enjoyed fairly good relations with the air base. Servicemen attended church and sporting events in the communities, hunted pheasants and were even invited into people's homes for meals. In addition, civilian personnel were essential at the base and worked in numerous capacities. Civilians even had their own section in The Duster to keep them informed of issues pertaining to their departments. They worked in the post exchange, depot supply warehouses, the wood mill and more.

Perhaps one of the most exciting events to happen at the air base was the arrival of Hollywood film star Clark Gable. Gable, who had enlisted in the U.S. Army Air Forces and went to Officer Candidate School for thirteen weeks, was trained as an aerial gunner and photographer and was part of the First Motion Picture Unit. In April 1943, Gable arrived with his crew to be processed, sending female hearts aflutter, according to an article in the Lincoln Star: "Of course if you want to ask some of the Kearney Teachers' college co-eds how they feel about Lieut. Gable—that's your privilege—but be sure that you take plenty of time out for waiting while they attempt to regain their breath and try to find the words to express their deep and very genuine admiration."[133] Another Hollywood celebrity, Anna May Wong, visited the base in December 1943.

A deadly accident occurred in early February 1944 when a plane crashed while taking off, engulfing the plane in flames. Six crew members were killed, two were seriously injured and two others escaped without injury.[134] One of the seriously injured fliers later succumbed to his injuries.[135]

As was popular at other air bases around Nebraska, the Kearney servicemen organized sports teams and played other air bases. Recreation activities were plentiful, including big band concerts and dances sponsored by the USO and by the 700th Army Air Forces Band. Some of the biggest names in the music industry also performed at the base, including Duke Ellington, Tommy Dorsey, the King Cole Trio and Les Brown and His Band of Renown. The base also had a bowling alley and a movie theater.

The 824th WAC (Women's Army Corps) unit arrived in June 1943 and lived on the base. Like other squadrons on base, it had its own section in The Duster to inform others of its activities. The unit took great pride in decorating its mess hall, painting the walls turquoise to pair with the flowered curtains.[136] Individual WACs were also profiled in The Duster, but the squadron received special attention in the newsletter when its new tropical beige uniforms came in that the GIs had "been casting lingering glances at."[137] WACs performed several key services around the base, from driving jeeps in the motor pool to delivering mail, performing office duties and being military police.

The arrival of V-E Day in May 1945 only briefly interrupted base activities, but there was a month-long push to contribute to the Seventh War Loan since the defeat of Japan still hung in the balance. Civilian and military personnel alike responded to the call.

After Japan was defeated, the air base gradually began to reduce personnel. The December 14, 1945 issue of The Duster led with the headline, "KAAF Becoming Shadow of Former Self." The WAC squadron was gone by the end

Black servicemen enjoy a respite from military duties and gather around a piano to sing, probably at the servicemen's club on Avenue A in Kearney. Kearney Army Air Base. Buffalo County Historical Society Trails and Rails Museum.

of the month, and other squadrons had consolidated due to the vast number of personnel being discharged or assigned to other air bases. The base would continue to be part of the U.S. Air Force and became the 27th Fighter Wing in July 1947. In March 1949, the Wing was transferred to a base in Texas, and the Kearney Army Air Force Base officially closed.[138]

The base left an indelible mark on the city of Kearney, bringing it challenges and opportunities.

LINCOLN ARMY AIRFIELD

If one lived in Lincoln during the war, it would have been nearly impossible to ignore the presence of the army air base located a few miles from the city. Local newspapers carefully tracked the base's happenings, from its original construction and the announcement of commanding officers to promotions and sports coverage. Every week, the Lincoln Star ran a special section of material from the army's public relations office, keeping not only the soldiers in the loop but the Lincoln community as well. The base and the community enjoyed good relations for the duration of the war, bringing a spark of excitement and purpose to Lincoln citizens. Civilian personnel working at the base numbered well over two thousand.

The base, designated by the U.S. Army Corps as a technical school, was located at the Lincoln Airport north of town. The U.S. War Department placed a notice in the lobby of the Lincoln Post Office on March 31, 1942, to announce the opening of bids for a new air mechanics school, even though Washington had not sent official approval of the project.[139] But the city council had faith and was soon rewarded when construction officially began in April 1942. Building proceeded rapidly, and the base was completed ahead of schedule.

Colonel Early E.W. Duncan, a North Carolina native, was named commander of the air base in April and arrived that same month to oversee construction and planning. He worked closely with the leaders of the community, even meeting with the chamber of commerce on May 11 where he stated, "I expect Lincoln to help with the Air Base." The chamber responded with a full-page ad addressed to Duncan in the Lincoln Sunday Journal and Star and wholeheartedly embraced its mission: "We are now united in a common cause which supersedes all other interests, and it is our pledge to work shoulder to shoulder with you and your associates to the end that the Lincoln Air Base may measure up to its solemn obligation to the national welfare."[140]

Soldiers began arriving at the base in May, and it was officially activated on May 18, 1942. Although the base was not yet completed, accommodations had been built for the soldiers, and the first classes began on July 6. Airmen were trained "in the inspection and maintenance of fighter airplanes, engines, and accessories." By November 1942, five classes had already graduated from the school—a total of 4,287 men.[141]

Construction moved rapidly and was completed August 29, 1942, weeks ahead of schedule. In addition to the barracks, the base included a bank, a post office, hangars, shops, a hospital, a school, houses and a fire station. Chapels were also built. All in all, 921 structures were constructed.[142] Similar to other large army air bases around Nebraska, it functioned like a small town with the appropriate necessities. Throughout its history, the base would serve several different purposes simultaneously:

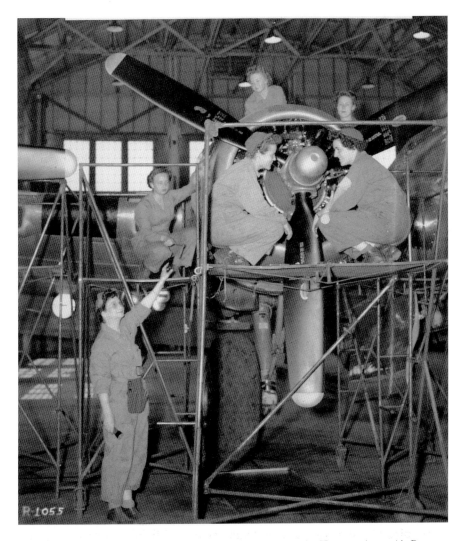

Women's Army Corps (WAC) mechanics work on a plane at the Kearney Army Air Base. Buffalo County Historical Society Trails and Rails Museum.

The 331st Army Air Force Base Unit commanded the support elements at Lincoln AAF as part of Air Technical Service Command, which was assigned to the 21st Bombardment Wing. It was also the home of the 12th Heavy Bombardment Processing Headquarters. The 616th Flying Training Group provided flying training instruction to aircrews of B-17 Flying Fortresses, Consolidated B-24 Liberators and Boeing B-29 Superfortresses. The 54th Training Sub-Depot provided indoctrination and basic training for 30,000 combat personnel; providing basic flight training for Army aviation cadets, and being a military separation center. The 604th Training Group provided instruction to over 25,000 aircraft mechanics, specializing in Fighter aircraft.[143]

But unlike some other air bases in Nebraska, morale never appeared to be an issue. An inspection report from November 1942 stated, "Morale at the Base is at an extremely high level"; the soldiers' demeanor was so extraordinary that the base was placed in the first six military camps in the United States for having "the best ratings in the deportment of the soldiers on the reservation." Most of these figures were based on the decrease in the number of social diseases and court-martials.[144]

As a technical school, the base was also open to training airmen from other Allied nations. Mexico, Peru, Brazil and the "Fighting French" government sent airmen to Lincoln. The base surpassed the language barrier by supplying interpreters. Most of these foreign nationals did well at the school and went on to contribute to the fight against the Axis powers.[145]

Due to a shortage of instructors, women were employed at the technical school as teachers. However, not many women met the mechanical knowledge required to teach. About eighty women taught at the school in March 1943, but this number steadily declined as several of the positions required "strenuous application" with heavy equipment or outdoor instruction; many of the women were assigned to other branches of instruction. By October 1943, only thirteen women instructors remained.[146]

Shortly after the first soldiers arrived on the base, women from the U.S. Army Nurses Corp arrived and, by November 1943, numbered eighty-two in all. The Lincoln Sunday Journal and Star profiled the many duties of these nurses in its October 25, 1942 issue, educating the citizens of Lincoln on these women's important role at the air base. Indeed, the hospital was also noted for the skill of its doctors in another feature story in the Nebraska State Journal. Colonel Cleveland Stewart, commander of the hospital, noted, "We have about the best qualified staff of any you would expect to accumulate at a hospital of this kind."[147]

The Special Services Department worked closely with civic organizations in Lincoln in order to provide a social life in Lincoln for servicemen. Only too happy to collaborate, these organizations, such as the Community Chest, immediately set up activities for the airmen. In August 1942, several Lincoln citizens invited airmen into their homes, thereby building a strong relationship between the base and the community from the very start. In addition, Lincoln citizens donated furniture, books, games and more to fill the dayrooms at the base itself.[148]

Unlike other smaller bases around Nebraska, the Lincoln Air Base boasted a vast amount of entertainment and social activities for the airmen. The service club served as the social center of the base, and a large theater and the sports arena hosted a variety of activities, from big band orchestras to dances, shows, films and sporting events such as basketball and boxing. To help keep morale high, the department rigged a piano to an army truck and called it the Morale Singing Program, driving around the base during different training exercises and engaging soldiers in singalongs.[149]

The base also had a well-stocked library. Thanks to the efforts of the Lincoln Public Library and the Victory Book Campaign, it received one thousand books, with the 7th Service Command sending along another two thousand. Originally housed in an unused section of the base exchange, the base built an entirely new library, complete with furniture, magazine subscriptions and more, and it enjoyed robust use. Nearly twenty-three thousand patrons used the library for reading and studying from January through October 1943 alone.[150]

Black soldiers came to the base in December 1943 to begin training to fly B-26 Marauders. For the black service men and women already

WACs take a stroll in downtown Kearney. Buffalo County Historical Society.

located in Lincoln, a USO Center opened for them in October 1943. According to an article in the Lincoln Sunday Journal and Star, the club had everything ready but the Venetian blinds hung for their opening date. Equipped with a jukebox, checkers, ample dancing space, ping pong tables, a writing center and a reading room, it was located at 212 South Twelfth Street and was equal to the USO space for white service men and women.[151] The club was perhaps opened at this date to prepare for famed black boxer Joe Louis's upcoming stop at the Lincoln Air Base for an exhibition boxing match.[152] The Urban League of Lincoln, an African American group, participated in several activities for the black soldiers. Urban League girls often went to dances at the black USO center and held parties and carnivals.

Not only did the air base host exhibition sporting matches, but it also participated in numerous sporting events with teams of its own. Baseball, basketball and boxing matches with other Nebraska air base teams occurred throughout the year, and local papers provided coverage while citizens from Lincoln and surrounding areas came as spectators.

Two women pose in front of a War Savings Bond sign. Kearney Army Air Base. Buffalo County Historical Society.

After the war ended, the air base served as a military separation center for those aircrews returning from overseas. It closed in December 1945 and was returned to the city of Lincoln. Today, one of the chapels, the Immanuel Temple Apostolic Holiness Church, is listed in the National Register of Historic Places.

McCook Army Airfield

Located nine miles northwest of the small town of McCook, the land here was selected in September 1942 to become an army airfield. The base officially opened in April 1943 and was under the command of the 2nd Air Force Headquarters in Colorado Springs, Colorado. The 520th Operational Training Unit operated here, and its main purpose was to provide final training for the B-17 Flying Fortress, Consolidated B-24 Liberator and Boeing B-29 Superfortress heavy bomber crews. In addition, crews trained in celestial navigation, gunnery, bombing communications, radar and aircraft maintenance.

As in other locations, McCook also dealt with a shortage of housing due to the influx of workers, civilians and military personnel. About 110 buildings were constructed at the base, including warehouses, barracks, a base theater, a fire station, a gymnasium, a hospital, a post office and more. Over the course of the base's existence, about five hundred civilians and fifteen thousand servicemen were stationed here.

But even as late as May 1944, the housing situation hadn't been relieved, even with the addition of "tent cities." One of the biggest problems at the field was the road between McCook and the base itself. In the official narrative history report, the highway's poor condition not only affected employment prospects but also contributed to a shortage of work hours. "Around 6,000 man hours were lost due to impassable roads," the report stated.[153] One month later, no action had yet been taken to repair the road. The high turnover rate of civilian personnel was a direct result of these two factors: the poor road and the housing difficulties.

However, morale remained high and was helped by the various activities offered by the service club. Bingo, ping pong tournaments, dances, sporting events, movies and concerts all contributed to this positive atmosphere, as well as the continuous work provided by the arrival of new "ships" (i.e., aircraft). The band at the base also often provided free concerts for the citizens of McCook.

Two fatal crashes occurred with airmen from the McCook air base. The first happened on May 5, 1944, near Scottsbluff, Nebraska, when a B-24J plane on a gunnery mission crashed. Six out of the eight-man crew were killed. The second fatal crash occurred on April 10, 1945, when a plane crashed near Maywood and killed five of the ten-man crew.

In addition to flight training, one of the main training objectives at McCook was work on the Norden bombsight, a highly classified instrument used in aerial warfare. At McCook, it was kept in a zippered bag in a "fortified storage building" (a vault) and was under constant guard. When used for training missions, a group of guards would escort it to the plane and give it to the bombardier. After the plane returned, guards would again put it in the zippered bag and march it back to the vault.[154]

In February 1945, the flight training program moved toward preparing for the conditions over the islands of Japan. An observation analyst of the 20th Air Force spoke to members of the 331st Bomb Group and emphasized the importance of radar training due to the relatively few clear days of the month in the skies above Japan suitable for bombing missions. But training for these conditions was made more difficult since the weather in the Nebraska skies offered only a limited number of days suitable for training missions at thirty thousand feet.[155] This, combined with the constant shortage of aircraft, made it difficult to complete the required training hours.

Buildings on county road DR 723 northwest of DR 381 at McCook Army Airfield. The small concrete structure in the foreground is the Second-Generation Norden Bombsight Vault, which is listed in the National Register of Historic Places. Wikimedia Commons.

The arrival of V-E Day only made it clear just how important it was to keep working toward the war's end. As recorded in the general history of the base, the day itself was nothing out of the ordinary. "It was a cold, dreary day; not the sort of day one reads about for such an occasion. There were no bells ringing, no horns blowing, no warm sun streaming down. It was just another work day closer to total victory. And yet it seemed appropriate. It seemed as if that was the sort of day for it to come on." Civilians and military alike stood in formation at an outdoor ceremony to mark the occasion, and a B-29 flew overhead as Colonel Kane spoke about the defeat of Germany and, now, the need to focus on defeating Japan. "We marched away," the report stated. "There was work to be done. We were getting ready for a total Victory."[156]

Although the crews kept training, by August 1945, their mission had come to an end with the defeat of Japan. The base officially closed on December 31, 1945. Today, although the field is owned primarily by farmers and the Nebraska Bureau of Land Management, there are still some World War II–era buildings standing, including a Norden bombsight vault.

SCRIBNER ARMY AIRFIELD

The air base located between the two villages of Scribner and Hooper was literally built in the middle of corn country. In October 1942, the U.S. Army Air Corps selected the site for use as an airfield, and accordingly, fifteen farmers were ordered to abandon their property, amounting to 2,300 acres. According to a story in the Scribner Rustler, this land "had been averaging more than 60 bushels of corn an acre."[157] Fremont, with a population of 1,200 people, was the closest large town to the base. The base was a satellite of the Sioux City Army Air Base in Iowa under the command of the 2nd Air Force until November 1943, when it became an independent base and Ainsworth Army Air Field became its satellite base. The 701st Bomb Squadron of the 445th Bomb Group was stationed here, and the field's purpose was to train B-24s air crews. In addition, the 36th Fighter Group also trained in Republic P-47 Thunderbolts for bomber escort and interception from November 1943 through March 1944.

The base was small compared to some others in Nebraska, and it only had about four hundred personnel, including about twenty civilian personnel. Originally, about fifty-seven buildings were constructed, including a hospital, barracks, an officers' mess hall, a hangar, a control tower, warehouses and more. But when the field became an independent installation, more buildings were needed, and as a result, the base was reorganized, with some buildings even being moved and new ones constructed. Eventually, there were ninety-seven buildings on the base.[158]

One of the more intriguing aspects of this air base was its camouflage. The entire base was made to look like a farm, complete with dummy pigs and cows. According to the official history, the army used a special material to make the entire field look like a large field of grass, which made it blend in well with the surrounding countryside. Dummy buildings and simulated roads were constructed and trees planted, making it difficult to distinguish the base from nearby agricultural land. In fact, the 910th Engineer Detachment did such an outstanding job that airmen flying to the base for the first time had a difficult time spotting it. The engineers had to maintain this camouflage to match the changing seasons.[159] A story in the Fremont Tribune from August 27, 2011, noted, "A lone hangar was painted red to resemble a barn. Chicken wire, stuffed with green spun glass, was designed to look like trees. A steeple was put on another building and painted to resemble a church. A schoolhouse was built and included spun-glass children."[160]

Another particular note of interest at Scribner was the use of K-9 dogs to guard the base. An article in the November 3, 1943 issue of the Lincoln Journal Star noted that Sergeant James Franklin, a "full-blooded Navajo Indian from New Mexico and a horse breaker in civilian life," was chosen from the Scribner base personnel to go to Fort Robinson and train war dogs. The four dogs that returned with Franklin to help guard the base were two German shepherds, a chestnut retriever and a Labrador.[161]

In March 1944, the Scribner base was put on "standby," which meant it had to maintain "at a standard for activation on 30 day(s) notice."[162] Since more men were being sent overseas, the military began to reduce the number of men at these smaller fields, with the eventual goal of shutting them down altogether.[163] The base was officially closed on December 31, 1945, and the land was acquired by the State of Nebraska in 1946.

SCOTTSBLUFF ARMY AIRFIELD

In September 1942, Scottsbluff was chosen as a satellite air base of the Casper (Wyoming) Army Air Field. Located about four miles east of the

An aerial view of the Scottsbluff Army Air Base. Legacy of the Plains Museum.

Servicemen pose in front of a B-17. Scottsbluff Army Air Base. Legacy of the Plains Museum.

Left: An unidentified mechanic poses in front of a B-17 plane called The Virginian. Scottsbluff Army Air Base. Legacy of the Plains Museum.

Below: Service men and women enjoy a dance probably at the base's recreation hall. Scottsbluff Army Air Base. Legacy of the Plains Museum.

Opposite, top: The headquarters building at the Scottsbluff Army Air Base. Legacy of the Plains Museum.

Opposite, middle: A hangar at the Scottsbluff Army Air Base. The insignia is that of the U.S. Army Air Forces. Legacy of the Plains Museum.

Opposite, bottom: The barracks at the Scottsbluff Army Air Base. Legacy of the Plains Museum.

Above: An unidentified man poses on the hood of a gas truck. Scottsbluff Army Air Base. Legacy of the Plains Museum.

Left: Airman Lou Towater poses with his flying gear at the Scottsbluff Army Air Base. Legacy of the Plains Museum.

Airmen enjoy some time off. From left to right: Hans Holtorf, Bill Harris, unidentified airman, Ethan Eckbird and Leland Robinson. Scottsbluff Army Air Base. Legacy of the Plains Museum.

town, nearly thirty farms had to be vacated in order to build the base, displacing families in the process. The 4190th Army Air Forces Base Unit was stationed here, and the base was used to train crews of Boeing B-17 Flying Fortresses and Consolidated B-24 Liberator bombers.

Construction proceeded rapidly, and once finished, the base included a hospital, barracks, hangars, a mess hall, officers' quarters, a bombsight storage building and more. The base was activated in December 1942. From January 1943 to August 1943, 156 crews were trained in one or more phases of training. During this time, these crews flew more than 3,400 missions. However, despite these numbers, the base was "short of everything, except hard work and a will to accomplish."[164]

According to the official base history, the citizens of Scottsbluff warmly welcomed the airmen. They opened a service center for them in town equipped with "furniture and a snack bar with coffee and cookies furnished free of charge." A group of women served as hostesses and junior hostesses at the dances held every night (accompanied by a jukebox) and then two dances a month with live music. They also helped the soldiers with their mending and other activities. A recreation hall at the base itself provided a place for airmen to relax and have parties, watch movies and more.[165]

To keep the airmen informed of base activities, military personnel published the Daily Bulletin. In addition to listing the "Officers of the Day" and other "military business," it also announced basketball and football games, listed the names of movies to be shown at the base theater and made special announcements, such as V-Mail stationery being available at the base post office or room vacancies in Scottsbluff, as well as service times for various church services, including Jewish, Catholic and Protestant.

In 1944, the base became a satellite base of the Alliance Army Airfield and the 1st Troop Carrier Demand. It shifted from training bomber crews to training C-47 and glider crews. It also performed radio and aircraft maintenance training.

The base closed in December 1945, and the land was turned over to the City of Scottsbluff in 1947. Nearly all of the original buildings were removed. Today, the Western Nebraska Regional Airport is located here.

Chapter 3

FORT ROBINSON AND THE WAR DOG TRAINING PROGRAM

Located in northwest Nebraska, Fort Robinson has been a fixture on the Pine Ridge since 1874. It played a pivotal role during the settling of the frontier and the Indian Wars. During World War II, it served as the location for a POW camp as well as a war dog training center.

In the years leading up to the war, Fort Robinson primarily served as a remount depot, training and caring for horses for the military. As the U.S. military increasingly became more mechanized in the years after World War I, the need for horses diminished, but there was still a necessity for them for various aspects of World War II. Horses were sent to the United States Coast Guard to patrol along the coastlines of New Jersey, Oregon and Washington, and they were also used for patrolling at prisoner of war camps. Horses were sent to army hospitals to help patients use riding therapy during their convalescence.[166]

Fort Robinson came under the jurisdiction of the 7th Service Command, and personnel, both civilian and military, increased in 1943. To handle the influx of new people, new buildings were erected, and every available location on the fort was used for living accommodations. Many soldiers lived in nearby Crawford or in Chadron, about twenty-eight miles away.

The fort was used for airborne maneuvers in August 1943. The 326th Glider Infantry and a battalion of the 507th Parachute Regiment came from the Alliance Airfield, in addition to the 253rd Field Artillery Battalion. The "Battle of Fort Robinson" occurred August 10–15, and gliders and planes filled the sky over the fort; more than 3,500 enlisted men and 100 officers participated. K-9 dogs from the fort's war dog training center also engaged in the mock battle. As Tom Buecker wrote, "The dogs and handlers served as sentries and scouts to locate airborne soldiers. An airborne colonel, who landed in a tree, was captured by a K-9 soldier and his dog. As K-9 soldier Robert Fisher remembered, 'The airborne troopers were surprised by the ferocity of the dogs and wouldn't have anything to do with them.'" Many of the troops who participated in this "battle" later participated in the Normandy invasion.[167]

A WAC detachment lived at Fort Robinson and filled many critical positions to relieve men for other duties. They worked in the motor pool, ran the filling station, hauled loads of salvage, served as secretaries, drove trucks and more. Romances did occur between the WACs and soldiers at Fort Robinson and often led to marriage.[168]

For entertainment, service clubs, USO shows, dances, sporting activities, movies and more were provided to those at the fort. Nearby Crawford, which had long enjoyed a close and sometimes tumultuous relationship with the fort, also served as a place for relaxation and entertainment.

After the war ended, the fort continued to operate as a remount depot, though not at the same levels previously known. The POW camp did not officially close until May 1946. The fort ceased to become a part of the U.S. Army in late 1949 and was transferred to the U.S. Department of Agriculture. Today, the fort is a state park, and thousands of tourists visit it every year.

THE WAR DOGS OF FORT ROBINSON

Perhaps one of the most intriguing World War II activities at Fort Robinson was the war dog training center. With its rugged terrain, pine-covered buttes and its longtime use as a remount depot, the fort was an ideal location for training dogs to fight in World War II.

Although dogs have been used in warfare since ancient times for their acute senses, training ability, devotion to man, speed, agility and vigilance, the United States did not have an official war dog training program until World War II. Even after Pearl Harbor, the War Department needed a little coaxing to make the program a reality. Arlene Erlanger, a nationally known dog exhibitor and breeder from New York, was way ahead of the War Department. Familiar with how other countries had used dogs in warfare in the past, Erlanger recognized the potential advantage of a war dog program for the United States and set about making it happen. Several phone calls and meetings later, the Dogs for Defense program was created in January 1942 and chaired by Harry I. Caesar, director of the American Kennel Club. The group began contacting dog clubs and obedience trainers around the nation and asked for their assistance in the new program. Many readily agreed.

Almost simultaneously, the Quartermaster Corps division of the U.S. Army realized the overwhelming need for sentry dogs to help patrol war plants and war supply depots. The potential threat of sabotage, especially on American coasts, was now a very real possibility. However, the military had never done a full-scale program of training sentry dogs. It took another civilian group to bring the army and the Dogs for Defense program together. The American Theater Wing, a group of performers known for entertaining the troops during World War I, wanted to contribute to the war effort and asked the military what it could do. The Quartermaster Corps thought that the American Theater Wing might be the very organization to help procure and train the dogs, but the Wing did not have the facilities for such a mission. Theater Wing actress Helen Menken, a lifelong dog lover, heard of Mrs. Erlanger's dog training efforts and contacted her.

With the blessing of the secretary of war, the Quartermaster Corps approached Dogs for Defense in February 1942 and asked it to procure and train dogs for sentry purposes. The Dogs for Defense leaders enthusiastically agreed, and on March 13, 1942, dogs were officially inducted into the U.S. Army. Since the program was new and thus experimental, finding the best way to train dogs and figuring out what duties they would best be suited for—besides sentry positions—took time. The only way dogs had officially been used in the U.S. military was as sled dogs. After three months of research, the Dogs for Defense program decided to initially train sentry dogs. It asked dog clubs and breeders, as well as their supporting partners, the Professional Handlers Association and the American Kennel Club, for assistance in acquiring two hundred dogs. It asked for donations to help defray costs and kennels for training purposes. Erlanger and Caesar also put up their own money to help finance the project.

Unfortunately, problems arose. The kennel locations used weren't big enough to train so many dogs, and instructors inexperienced in training sentry dogs added another complication. To fix these problems, the army decided to put the program under the Remount Branch of the Quartermaster Corps in July 1942. This branch knew how to deal with large groups of animals since it managed the army's horses. The army also broadened the scope of the war dog program by adding training for not only sentry work but also messenger, wire-laying, first aid, scouting, attacking and trail work. The Army Ground Forces and the Army Air Forces were ordered to "explore the possibilities of using dogs advantageously in the various activities under their control." Orders also included establishing programs in how to train handlers and improve training practices. In addition, the army wanted to make sure there were training facilities that were big enough to expand if the program proved to be beneficial. This new strategy meant that Dogs for Defense no longer trained dogs but, instead, was responsible for acquiring them.

In August 1942, training facilities, called War Dog Reception and Training Centers, were set up at already existing Remount Depots in locations across the country, including Fort Robinson.[169] The fort was an excellent location for a K-9 training center because of its rugged landscape (perfect for training dogs for war), two major railroad lines and a central location. Construction began in September 1942 in an area north of the fort's warehouse area and included a K-9 hospital, a conditioning and isolation building, classroom and training buildings, an obstacle course nicknamed the "Crazy Horse Run," barracks for the trainers and the rest of those involved with the project and 1,800 kennels.[170]

The training center was activated on October 3, 1942, and the first dogs arrived in Fort Robinson that same day; by December 31, 1,070 dogs had been received.[171] Once the dogs arrived, they were examined by a veterinarian and then put in quarantine for two weeks to ensure that they were free from disease. And then, like their human counterparts, they went through basic training for about one month.

Trainers' days started early, at 5:30 a.m. Before they began training the dogs, these men went through two weeks of classroom instruction and learned how to care for the dogs' health and manage their kennels, as well as dog psychology. After those two weeks, the men began training with the dogs for about forty-five minutes per day.[172] The dogs learned how to obey gestures and verbal commands, grew used to wearing gas masks and muzzles, learned to ride in vehicles and also became accustomed to gunfire. Making sure that the dogs and their handlers were trained together as a team was integral to success, especially in terms of tactical or sentry work. One man to four dogs served as the best ratio for training purposes.[173]

A peek at the "Notes for the Handling, Feeding, and Care of War Dogs" document shows just how important it was for the trainer and the dog to work together as a team. "The performance of the war dog unfailingly reflects the work habits and the attitudes of the master. If the master is exact, energetic, and 'on the job,' the dog will be the same. If the man is slothful and careless, the dog will, in time, acquire the same characteristics."[174] The relationship between dog and master became very close.

After basic training, dogs were evaluated and then assigned to specialized training duties for eight to twelve weeks based on their aptitudes. Sentry dogs required the least training, while those dogs with "exceptional qualifications" were trained as combat patrol scouts and message carriers. With the exception of the messenger dog, all K-9s needed an attitude of aggression since they were trained to spot trouble. In contrast, loyalty was the trait most desired for messenger dogs. They wanted to please their masters more than anything.

An example of the specifications needed for certain duties can be found in the "Introductory Notes and Instructions for Training War Dogs" document.

A trainer and handler work at dog agitation with a German shepherd at the Fort Robinson War Dog Training Center. Circa 1944. RG2731.PH000005-000010. Used with permission from History Nebraska.

A trainer works at dog agitation with a collie at the Fort Robinson War Dog Training Center. Circa 1944. RG2731.PH000005-000004. Used with permission from History Nebraska.

Mobile patrol dogs required "silence in working, highly developed scenting powers, aptitude for training, acute hearing and quick reaction, good eyesight, physical fitness, and free from gun-shyness (getting used to explosions)." The guidelines then outlined a scenario to "test" the dog to see if it possessed these qualities. If the dog did not meet the minimum qualifications, then "little or no success can be expected."[175]

When training was completed, it was time for dog and master to show their stuff. Sentry dogs were assigned to military installations all around the United States. These included coastal defenses, airfields, arsenals, ammunition dumps and even industrial plants. The threat of Hitler's U-boats and Japanese submarines along the Pacific and Atlantic coasts meant nonstop work for the sentry dogs with the Coast Guard beach patrols. Sentry dogs were also used in the nearby POW camp at Fort Robinson, and some of the prisoners themselves worked at the K-9 training center.

Fort Robinson had become the major dog training center in the United States by October 1944, with all other dog training centers around the United States closing. Since its opening, the center had trained 3,565 dogs,

Five men and three dogs are visible, training in the wood reserve with snow on the ground at the Fort Robinson War Dog Training Center. Circa 1944. RG2731.PH000006-000020. Used with permission from History Nebraska.

with 1,353 dogs "on hand." Due to the success of the Normandy invasion in June 1944 and the decrease of German domination over the Atlantic, there was an increased need to train scout dogs for use in the Pacific theater of war. Thus, most training activities focused on this.[176]

This type of training differed from what they'd typically been doing. Jungle density made it difficult to see, with vision limited to only a few feet, but with a dog's superior sense of smell and hearing, they would be able to "locate unfamiliar animals and men."[177] In the spring of 1943, the War Department General Staff decided to see how a detachment of six scout and two messenger dogs would do in the Pacific. Fortunately, the reports that came back were positive. Animals were put in the forward and combat areas with reconnaissance patrols and did an excellent job of detecting the presence of Japanese soldiers up to a range of one thousand yards, depending on certain conditions like wind direction and terrain type. Other reports were also favorable.[178] Thus, by June 1945, with the war in Europe over and scout dogs having been found capable of doing the job, all training focused on scout dogs. Six platoons were organized and trained at Fort Robinson for this specific duty. Tom Buecker described this training as follows:

> Duringthetwelve-weektrainingperiod,themenandthedogsreceived atleast10hoursof intenseinstruction,muchof theworkcenteringon reconnaissancepatrols,wherethesilentscoutdogshadalreadyproven themselves.Thehandlerworkedwiththedogonaleash,usuallyatthe pointoralongsideapatrol,dependingonthewind.Scoutdogsalsowere trainedtodetecttheapproachof anenemyorattemptedinfiltrationof anoutpost.Inthisroletledogswereespeciallyvaluablefornightguard, becausetheycouldgivethehandlersilentwarningof theenemylongbefore humans were aware of any danger.[179]

But just as the training ended for the scout dogs, the war ended in Japan. Nevertheless, the trainers and their dogs still went through a graduation ceremony. Arlene Erlanger, who'd started the Dogs for Defense program, was a special guest. Following the ceremony, there were dog demonstrations and other entertainment for the crowd to enjoy.[180] After all, who doesn't enjoy watching well-trained dogs showing off their admirable skills?

Indeed, because the Dogs for Defense program had been a national one, interest in the K-9 training center at Fort Robinson was national as well. Throughout the training center's existence, national magazines such as LIFE and National Geographic visited the center and wrote stories, while Paramount, the Hollywood movie company, and the U.S. Signal Corps filmed training sequences for newsreels. Dogs appeared in local parades and celebrations, and there were several open houses for the general public to attend. Official visitors came to see the training program, and letters poured in from across the country from dog owners whose dogs were stationed at the fort. An eleven-year-old asked, "I would like to know if I can put a star in my window because I gave you my dog. When does he get a rating?"[181]

After the war ended, sadly, not all dogs returned. Many gave their lives to protect their handlers and the soldiers and marines they guarded, while others succumbed to diseases or died due to accidents. The Quartermaster Corps had to demobilize the K-9s and return them to their civilian owners. But it promised not to return them unless they were fit for civilian life once again. The dogs went through a "demilitarizing" process that included thorough obedience training and a series of tests. If the dogs passed the tests, they were offered to their original owners if the owners wanted them returned. Only a fraction of dogs were unfit to be returned and were usually euthanized. Some handlers, having grown very attached to their dogs, were able to keep them.[182]

By December 1945, the training center had "received 11,437 dogs for training. Of that number, 4,889 were successfully trained and issued, while 5,300 had been rejected or discharged and returned to their owners. Only 640 dogs and 77 enlisted men remained at the center." Although the center was officially deactivated in June 1945, the remaining dogs were used in rescue missions in Colorado and Wyoming. By June 1947, the last of the dogs were sold to a former sled dog training officer at Fort Robinson, and the center was officially closed.[183]

Overall, the experimental war dogs program proved to be a success, showing the American military and the American population alike what many dog enthusiasts already knew: a dog could save lives and be an integral part of winning the war. Their unwavering loyalty to their handlers made them invaluable.

Chapter 4

THE SCRAP DRIVE

Henry Doorly's Nebraska Plan

For many Nebraskans who grew up during the war years, the scrap drives often bring back fond memories. Children pulled their red wagons around the neighborhood to collect scrap, farmers dug through weeds to find outdated implements and housewives chucked used pots and pans onto the scrap pile. Even Hollywood got in on the act. Daffy Duck's animated film Scrap Happy Daffy showed him protecting the scrap heap from a Nazi Billy goat, while a poster featuring Mickey Mouse and Pluto proclaimed, "Get in the scrap!" Every American, young and old, could participate and feel good about contributing to the war effort.

Nebraska, however, holds a special place in the historical narrative. The Nebraska Plan, developed by Henry Doorly, publisher of the Omaha World-Herald, was put into action in July 1942 with a statewide competition to see which county could collect the most scrap. It proved such a remarkable success that the U.S. government decided to adopt the plan nationwide largely because in the months before Nebraskans made a national name for themselves, the scrap drives sponsored by the United States government had decidedly lackluster results. Doorly's ingenuity and marketing savvy proved a winning combination, but it was Nebraskans who really stepped up to the plate. During the three weeks of the competition in 1942, Nebraskans collected a staggering sixty-seven thousand tons of scrap. The state inspired the rest of America to "Salvage for Victory" for the remainder of the war.

A Scrap Shortage?

In December 1941, Scientific American ran an article on the "threat of a serious shortage of steel scrap material." Because of the boost in national defense production, officials worried that they would not have enough scrap to keep the steel furnaces running, and the very thought caused "deep concern." Since the United States was also building war materiel for the Lend-Lease program and now had to focus on defense production for America, it was right to worry. Even this early in the war, steel companies tried to rustle up scrap. They appealed to employees and the communities where their plants were located, but to little avail.[184]

The government also recognized the potential disaster waiting to happen if war production ground to a halt and decided to set up another committee to deal with the problem. In January 1942, Executive Order 9024 gave the War Production Board the authority to "direct procurement of materials and industrial production programs."[185] As James Kimble wrote, the board had a difficult time coming up with a workable campaign to convince Americans to turn in their scrap for the war effort. The bureaucratic red tape frustrated many Americans. Others didn't want to part with their so-called scrap (i.e., old farm implements or machinery), due to the possibility of future rationing programs. The previous campaigns had failed miserably. The issue continued to snowball, and even President Roosevelt became alarmed, writing to a U.S. representative that "we anticipate that the scrap shortage may become more acute during the winter of 1942–1943."[186]

Such dire news continued to fill newspapers and magazines throughout the nation, and in 1942, when the United States military was flailing, something clearly needed to be done to galvanize Americans into turning in their scrap and assisting the war effort. And in Omaha, one Nebraskan came up with the solution.

Henry Doorly and the Nebraska Plan

As James Kimble detailed in his well-researched book on the Nebraska scrap drive, Prairie Forge: The Extraordinary Story of the Nebraska Scrap Metal Drive of World War II, Henry Doorly determined how he could assist the scrap drive due to a well-timed question from his wife, Margaret. In July 1942, after reading the news on how FDR had decided to extend the rubber salvage drive due to its abysmal results, he found himself grumbling. Margaret simply asked, "What did you do about it?" Doorly—an immigrant, newspaper owner, husband and father—took the question seriously. Within the next few days, he pondered what he could do to help light a fire in his fellow Americans to turn in their scrap. Soon, he and his staffers developed a plan and put it into action, giving his employees only ten days to make it happen.[187] Doorly and his staff implemented a winning strategy, but it included a massive amount of organization. With the help of the state salvage director, Mark Caster, Omaha World-Herald employees coordinated with all ninety-three Nebraska counties to prepare them for the upcoming scrap drive. They created promotional materials, contacted daily and weekly Nebraska newspapers and worked with the governor's office. It was an impressive feat.

What made the plan unique, however, was its competitive nature and its focus on the homefront as a "vital part" of the war effort.[188] County would compete against county, with prizes of war bonds for first- and second-place competitors. The advertising didn't just focus on farm implements, but rather encompassed household goods, junk stuck in attics and every other kind of scrap available from every Nebraskan. "Simply put," Kimble wrote, "citizens young and old were asked to search for everything with metal content that could be scrapped for the war effort."[189]

Doorly unveiled his plan in a radio broadcast on four Omaha radio stations the evening of Saturday, July 11, 1942. In his speech, he addressed how too many Americans had indulged in "wishful thinking" that the Allies' minor victories would soon translate into major ones without any help from the average American people. Why, as long as defense industries built more munitions than the enemy, all would be well. "Don't you believe it," Doorly intoned. "We are fighting the most ruthless, murderous and efficient combination of armed forces the world has known." Doorly condemned complacency and appealed to Nebraskans to be individually responsible for doing their part and then talked about the scrap shortage, laying the blame for it squarely on those Americans who did not bother to turn their scrap in to the government. But he had a solution, and Nebraskans would lead the charge. "Well, I propose to the people of Nebraska that we show the rest of the nation what can be done by an aggressive, fighting state that is alive to its responsibilities....The nation needs your help now. You personally need it, for you are part of the nation that will go down if we fail to win this war."[190]

The challenge had been issued. Now it was up to Nebraskans to accept it.

In the coming days, the Omaha World-Herald published the rules of the competition, which ran from July 19 to August 8, 1942. Every Nebraskan "living in a county" was eligible, including youth organizations such as 4-H clubs, Boy Scouts, Girl Scouts and so on. Each county's salvage committee would be in charge of the program, and it would provide receipts, issued in pounds of scrap submitted, for all salvage at "point of entry." At the end of every day, an Omaha World-Herald correspondent would telegraph the Omaha paper and give them the total of the previous day's collection. These totals would be published in the Omaha World-Herald on a daily basis so that each county could see their standings. This also increased competition. Prizes ranged from first place, "$1,000 in war bonds to be given to the charity of its choice," to $50 in war bonds for the junior club winner. In addition, people were encouraged to wear badges that stated, "Scrap Scout: I brought in 25 lbs."[191]

The competition was on, and Nebraskans took it seriously, as did Nebraska industries, including the Union Pacific Railroad and the Burlington Railroad. An article in the July 25, 1942 issue of the Omaha World-Herald stated, "Fired by the competitive American spirit, virtually every town in the state is making a vigorous effort to see that its county ranks well at the top in the Nebraska salvage contest." In Chadron, seven planes were set to drop leaflets on the town to inform residents about the scrap drive, and these same types of "bombs" were also dropped over Auburn and Peru. In Neligh, the World War I cannon, an Austrian 77, that had been on the courthouse lawn since 1920, was a casualty of the scrap drive, as was a four-ton souvenir cannon from Valentine.[192] A cannon used in the Spanish-American War, ostensibly made during the time of the American Revolution, sat on the University of Nebraska campus in Lincoln for forty-five years until it, too, fell victim to the scrap drive.[193]

Many towns also had their own prize packages and incentives. In North Platte, the law firm of Beatty, Maupin and Murphy offered a prize of a twenty-five-dollar war bond to the two citizens of Lincoln County who contributed the most scrap to the contest. During a pep rally in Albion, it was announced that forty dollars in prizes would be awarded to the largest scrap collections for both individual and groups. A slightly different contest occurred in Western. Anyone who donated scrap had a chance to try to "crack" a large safe donated by C. Urbach.[194]

Throughout the next three weeks, newspapers across the state were filled with stories about the scrap drive. In Scotts Bluff County, July 31 was declared "scrap day," and Mayor Everett Dennis's declaration stated, in part, "I urge your fullest cooperation in our campaign. This is a patriotic undertaking and your patriotism should exceed the attraction of cash prizes…in an effort to serve our country in the greatest collection of vital materials possible." Boy Scouts would go door to door to businesses and homes to collect scrap, while 4-H clubs in rural areas would do the same.[195] A "scrap dance" was planned in Norfolk with a "certain number of pounds of scrap metal or rubber" as the admission fee. Washington County, which had done well in previous scrap drives (the ones organized by the federal government before the Nebraska Plan) decided that if it won any of the prize money from the Omaha World-Herald, it would be divided equally among the county's churches. In addition, it gave each of the county's 1,500 farms a quota of 350 pounds of scrap "despite the fact the harvest rush is on."[196]

The scrap drive even got a little bit of help from Hollywood. Comedy duo and film stars Bud Abbott and Lou Costello participated in Lincoln's Victory Day, riding in a jeep during the parade and then appearing at the capitol for a war bond rally, where Governor Griswold presented them with an ear of corn as a souvenir.[197] The pair then traveled to Omaha and caused quite a stir when they donned coveralls, hopped on a scrap truck and made their way through a few Omaha neighborhoods. At one, they stopped a fourteen-year-old boy and asked, "Where's that scrap you were going to give your Uncle Sam?" The boy confessed it was still at home, so Costello said, "Let's go then" and the trio dashed to the boy's apartment, returning with armfuls of scrap metal. The pair broadcast the entire adventure, using their usual slapstick routines, but at the end of their quest they said, "We aren't kidding anymore…we know we've been broadcasting on the most important program on the earth—congratulations, Nebraska."[198]

By July 31, the scrap drive contest had already collected 17 million pounds. Grant County in western Nebraska led the state, with Thayer and Red Willow Counties second and third, respectively.[199] The scrap drive had captured Nebraskans' attention, but that wasn't all. People throughout the country were watching the competition, and some even came to Nebraska to see it in action. C.C. Cohen, a director of the National Institute of Scrap and Steel in Kansas City, Missouri, visited Omaha at the end of July. "It's amazing what the public can do when it is provided the proper organization," he said.[200]

Although the competition lagged a bit after the first two weeks, the last week saw the Omaha World-Herald and Governor Griswold himself pushing Nebraskans to give their all. Several editorial cartoons and ads in the newspaper, some of them depicting Hitler and other Axis leaders, played more on patriotism than the friendly spirit of competition. After all, there was a war to be won. But the competition got a healthy jolt of motivation when Governor Griswold declared Friday, August 7, as Harvest Festival Day and August 8, the last day of the competition, as Farm Scrap Holiday in

A propaganda poster for the 13th Naval District, U.S. Navy, shows a snake representing Japan being bombed by an eagle and encourages Americans to turn in their scrap for the war effort. During the war, the use of the term "Jap" was common. However, today it is a racial slur. Library of Congress, POS—WPA—WASH .P45, no. 1.

Nebraska. The front page of the Omaha World-Herald announced the news, and in his speech, Griswold pushed Nebraskans to go the distance since the eyes of the nation were on them. "Nebraska, in a three weeks [sic] campaign, has aroused national interest in the effort of its people to show that scrap can be brought in to market quickly; but fine as our effort has been, the results must be much greater if this campaign is to succeed."[201]

It worked. Nebraskans responded to the challenge, and the pounds of scrap submitted per day went up dramatically. "In standings published on August 10, there was a 17-point jump over the previous day's average," Kimble wrote. "On the same day, the number of counties with individual averages over 100 pounds per person leapt from 18-28, and the reports were still coming in as the various county chairmen worked furiously to catch up from the late deluge of scrap."[202]

Everyone, young and old, rushed to meet the governor's challenge. It was no longer just a competition to see which county could win the grand prize— it had become something more. Nebraskans worked together, overcoming regional differences, to accomplish the task at hand, fueled by feelings of patriotism and the need to defeat the Axis. This was aptly demonstrated by the actions of an eight-year-old girl from Plattsmouth. Connie Rae McCaroll's brother, Don, had enlisted in the U.S. Air Corps before the scrap drive started. Don sent her a letter, along with a war bond, and wrote, "We have to have material for planes." Connie Rae didn't hesitate.

Sheimmediatelyletteredasignwithredandbluecrayon,anddecorated withanAmericanflag,whichread, "GiveYourOldIrontotheUseof America."Thisshepostedonatelephonepoleinfrontofherhome.Connie thenwentonascraphunt,enlistingtheaidofDelbertColwellwhoowned acoasterwagon.Theyaccompaniedtheloadofmetalwhichtheycollected to the city scales. It weighed 1,230 pounds.[203]

On the final night of the scrap drive, August 8, the city of Omaha held a bonfire in downtown Omaha. As Kimble wrote about that night, "Thousands of citizens were present for the occasion, and they listened avidly as George Grimes, one of Doorly's chiefs of scrap, told them that 'you and the other people of Nebraska have given the most amazing demonstration of loyalty and patriotic fervor.'" People in attendance were so moved by the speech that they jumped to their feet and sang the national anthem.[204]

Once the tallies were completed, the Omaha World-Herald announced the winner: Grant County. Its populace averaged "637.95 pounds for every one of its 1,327 residents."[205] Hooker County took second place, while Thomas County took third.

In the upcoming days and weeks, the news about the scrap drive resonated throughout America. The September 21, 1942 issue of LIFE featured a glowing review of the scrap drive, stating, "It was more than a scrap drive; it was a great resurgence of American folks hungry to go to war."[206] The White House certainly was aware of its success. The War Production Board knew that the Nebraska Plan could work nationwide, and it invited Doorly to Washington, D.C., along with two hundred newspaper publishers from around the country. The group worked quickly and came up with a new scrap drive initiative, the Newspapers' Scrap Metal Drive, which launched on September 28, 1942, and again lasted for three weeks. It closely followed Doorly's plan. Americans responded, just as Nebraskans had, and this time, even more celebrities participated, including Bing Crosby, Walt Disney, Rita Hayworth and Gene Autry. President Roosevelt even received scrap donations at the White House.[207]

In May 1943, the Omaha World-Herald won a Pulitzer Prize in the Public Service category. The prize stated, "For its initiative and originality in planning a state-wide campaign for the collection of scrap metal for the war effort. The Nebraska plan was adopted on a national scale by the daily newspapers, resulting in a united effort which succeeded in supplying our war industries with necessary scrap material."[208] Andrew Higgins, a Columbus native who moved to New Orleans and invented the Higgins boats, praised the paper for its effort. In Omaha that month to receive an honorary degree from Creighton University, Higgins said, "There's something unique about Nebraska and Nebraskans, their government, the way they have of doing things. If other states will follow the lead of Nebraska and the World-Herald we will have no scrap-iron problem."[209]

Although postwar analysis has concluded that there probably was not an urgent need for scrap, as there was never a shortage, hindsight is indeed 20/20. At the time, the U.S. government based its decision on the information available and acted accordingly. Since scrap was indeed a vital part of making munitions, it was necessary to the war effort. Nebraskans could certainly be proud of how they inspired the rest of the nation to sit up and take notice of the need for scrap and showed their fellow Americans exactly how to collect it and, in so doing, greatly boost civilian morale and patriotism. Were it not for Henry Doorly and the Nebraska Plan, the scrap drives might have had a very different outcome, one that could have had serious consequences on the war effort.

Chapter 5

NEBRASKA'S POW CAMPS

A s the war continued, prisoners of war inevitably became part of the picture. For the most part, German and Italian POWs were held in Great Britain in the early years of the war. But by June 1942, the prisoner population had swelled so much that Great Britain asked the United States for help. America agreed to shoulder the responsibility for 50,000 POWs. For the rest of 1942 and most of 1943, the Office of the Provost Marshal General created a POW camp system across the country. By the end of the war, the United States would house more than 450,000 POWs. Every state but two—Vermont and Nevada—had POW camps.

In Nebraska, there were three POW base camps—Camp Atlanta, located in Phelps County in south-central Nebraska; Fort Robinson, located in northwest Nebraska in Dawes County; and Camp Scottsbluff, located in Scotts Bluff County in the Panhandle of Nebraska. Camp Indianola originally began in the summer of 1943 as a base camp and then was converted to a branch camp of Camp Atlanta in May 1944; then it became a base camp in September 1944. It ended the war as a branch camp of Camp Atlanta. Camp Atlanta had about sixteen satellite or branch camps in the southern half of the state, as well as two in Kansas. Between 1944 and 1945, they included Grand Island, Hastings, Kearney, Franklin, Hebron, Weeping Water, Elwood, Bertrand, Alma, Lexington, Palisade, Ogallala, Benkelman, Hayes Center and Indianola. The two in Kansas were at Hays and Cawker City.[210] Camp Scottsbluff, the oldest of the three base camps, had prisoners arrive in June 1943 and had branch camps at Bridgeport, Bayard, Lyman, Mitchell and Sidney, as well as two in Wyoming, Veteran and Torrington.[211] Italian prisoners were briefly interned at Fort Crook in Sarpy County near Omaha. With the exception of Fort Robinson, these camps were almost entirely used for agriculture and contract labor purposes.[212] In the fall of 1944, Fort Robinson had three side camps in South Dakota.[213]

The War Department designed a basic construction and layout plan used in each camp. In Nebraska, Fort Robinson, Scottsbluff, Atlanta and Indianola were built from the ground up. For branch camps, POWs stayed in fairgrounds, tent cities and unused buildings. Each camp was required to follow the guidelines set forth in the Geneva Convention of 1929, to protect not only enemy POWs but also American prisoners of war held in Europe.

Major Maxwell S. McKnight of the OPMG's office outlined the camp layout as follows:

The basic feature of the plan is the compound. A camp consists of one or more compounds surrounded by two wire fences. Compounds are separated from each other by a single fence. Each compound houses four companies or prisoners or approximately 1,000 prisoners. The housing and messing facilities are equivalent to those furnished to United States troops at base camps as required by the Geneva Convention. These facilities consist of five barracks, a latrine containing showers and laundry tubs with unlimited hot and cold running water, a mess hall, and an administrative building for each company. In addition, each compound is provided with a recreation building, an infirmary, a workshop, a canteen building, and an administration building. The compound area is sufficient to provide outdoor recreation space. Each camp also has a chapel, a station hospital, and a large outdoor recreation area for the use of all prisoners at the camp. At some camps located on an Army post, certain wards of the post hospital are designated for the use of prisoners of war in lieu of a station hospital at the prisoner of war camp.[214]

The administration was composed of a central guard house, a main administration building and a tool house combined with an office. There were also "quartermaster offices, warehouses (including cold storage), shops, fire house, and other miscellaneous facilities specific to a particular project."[215] Camps often included a post office, a warehouse and a utility area. Some camps, like Fort Robinson, also included a bakery, a post exchange, a library and movie theater.[216] This layout was essentially the same for all camps throughout the United States. Building anything more substantial would have cost the army more time and money.

Officers and enlisted men usually did not live in the same camp, or if they did, they were segregated in separate commands and separate barracks. American guard personnel came from military escort companies (MPs). With the influx of POWs, the provost marshal general requested that more MP companies be activated so that there would be about three prisoners to each guard. Of course, this figure differed depending on how many prisoners were at each camp. Security also differed. Some camps used watch towers or watch dogs, while others used "four-man patrols within the compound."[217]

Nebraskans who lived near the camps watched the construction with a mixture of curiosity and fear. Who, exactly, were these prisoners? Were they really the menacing Nazis they saw in Hollywood movies and on propaganda posters?

Not exactly. Since Nazism was a political belief, not every German soldier in the military subscribed to Nazi ideology. Neither was every German soldier actually German. Instead, the German military machine consisted of men from Germany's allies; western, northern and eastern European nations; forced conscription; and even prisoners and concentration camp inmates from the Reich. Soldiers from every European country and the Soviet Union fought with the Germany army. This clash of cultures and ideals naturally created a problem for the German military, but when those men became prisoners of war, those problems took on a whole new significance within the camps.

As historian Antonio Thompson wrote:

> Little thought was given to the differences between the men in German uniform. Besides, what would it matter if Fritz or Hans came from Austria or Poland or was a Democratic Socialist or National Socialist? They were still German, still the enemy, and all Nazis. Aryan mythology aside, the prisoners came from across Europe and Asia. Brown-skinned and brown-eyed soldiers of every conceivable age mingled with the "Teutonic" blond-haired, blue-eyed "German" youth. Germans and non-Germans and Nazis and non-Nazis mixed with the ideologically unsuitable, socially undesirable, and physically and emotionally unreliable. Some of these warriors used to feed the Nazi war machine had little or no grasp of the German language. While the Americans considered the German soldiers a homogenous group, the men in German uniform always remained conscious of the distinction.[218]

Of course, Nebraskans remained largely unaware of these distinctions. Over the course of the next few years, however, many Nebraskans would develop a close working relationship with many of these men. The large German immigrant population in the state meant that many shared a common culture and language with German POWs. A small number of Italian prisoners also came to Nebraska, and Italian immigrants to the state enjoyed the same type of relationship.

The first prisoners of war to arrive in Nebraska came to Camp Scottsbluff in June 1943. Captured during the Northern African and Italian campaigns, these Italian prisoners of war made quite the impression in the Panhandle. They were young, between twenty and twenty-five, and cut a fine figure to the reporters who wrote of their arrival. "And they are powerful men—broad shouldered, trim waisted and with smooth, strong muscles rippling beneath well bronzed skins. They are hard and fit—that's why they have been able to throw off the fatigue which they might well be expected to feel after long months of desert fighting."[219] These Italian soldiers were from the elite Italian rifle and sharpshooter units known as the Bersaglieri. They wore distinctive black plumes on their helmets and earned an impressive reputation. As prisoners, though, they no longer wore their famous black plumes, but torn and tattered clothing. They were a proud bunch all the same.

Herb Hinman, whose family lived across the road from the POW camp, remembered sitting with his family on their front porch and watching the Italians march into camp. "They seemed to be happy, some whistling or singing as they walked along like they were going for a stroll," he remembered. "They would even wave and speak out as they went by until the guards spoke to them."[220]

German POWs arrived in Fort Robinson in November 1943 and in Camp Atlanta in January 1944. Both groups were captured in North Africa and included troops from Erwin Rommel's famed Afrika Korps. Sergeant Alfred Thompson, stationed at Fort Robinson, surreptitiously took a picture of the arriving Germans who came in on the train, disembarked at nearby Crawford, Nebraska, and marched the nearly five miles to the POW camp.

At every camp, the prisoners kept busy. They had access to a canteen where they could buy sweets and soda pop, paper for letter writing and more. Arts and crafts, sporting events (soccer and bocce ball were favorites), church services, participating in classes, watching movies, theater and orchestra productions and more broke what was otherwise dull monotony. Being a prisoner wasn't easy; loneliness, political disagreements with other prisoners, depression and more could make life very difficult for a POW.

Thus, when the U.S. government and the War Department started the labor program in 1943, many POWs jumped at the chance to go beyond the barbed wire and do physical work. With the labor shortage around the country, farmers and other Nebraskans were grateful for the help. Without it, crops would rot in the field. POWs were paid eighty cents per day in canteen coupons. Because of the labor program, branch camps popped up around Nebraska to help ease transportation issues and fuel consumption. Indeed, many farmers, after going through the difficult process of hiring POW labor, went to these branch camps to pick up POWs and take them back to the farm. At the beginning of the program, several guards accompanied the prisoners, but this eventually decreased to only one guard. Most POWs had no desire to escape. Many were astonished to realize how big America was, which meant returning to the Fatherland to fight wasn't nearly as easy as they thought.

However, some escapes did occur, though none was ultimately successful. In July 1943, Theodore Kogge, twenty-one, and Otto Koch, twenty-three, escaped from the Bridgeport branch camp. They escaped on a Friday and made it as far as Colorado before the FBI captured them that Sunday.[221] Two escapees from Scottsbluff evaded capture for several months. Karl Tomola, forty-six, and Wolfgang Kurzer, twenty-two, escaped on July 1, 1944, and weren't captured until that November. The pair made their way to Canada and worked on several farms before crossing back over to the United States in New York and then ending up in Philadelphia. The two snuck on board a Spanish ship and hid themselves in empty oil drums. A tip from one of the ship's sailors led the FBI to find the two men, who were found to have two weeks' worth of food, eight dollars and ten pounds of chocolate for their journey.[222] Prisoners who escaped were not returned to the original camps where they were held; instead, they were transferred to different ones.

Throughout the American POW camp system, political tensions within the camps could also make life dangerous for POWs. Those who retained their allegiance to Nazism usually controlled the camps, and POWs who pushed back and took an anti-Nazi stanch often found themselves the targets of violence. Men who translated and read American newspapers or who made anti-Nazi statements in the camp could find themselves beaten or worse. Many were put into protective custody or transferred to different camps. Unfortunately, despite this tactic, Nazism in the camps continued to worsen. Eventually, weeding out Nazis from the anti-Nazis became the tool of choice to control the violence. On July 17, 1944, a comprehensive directive from the War Department sought to solve the problem by segregating the Nazis from the anti-Nazis. All German army officer prisoners were to be separated from their noncommissioned officers and enlisted men and put into either the anti-Nazi camp at Camp Ruston, Louisiana, or to the pro-Nazi camp at Camp Alva, Oklahoma. German NCOs were isolated at camps designated for their service command. For the 7th Service Command, in which all Nebraska camps fell, they were to be transferred to Camp Clark, Missouri.[223]

Unfortunately, the violence continued. The War Department decided to try something radically different: reeducation. If German POWs could understand the benefits of democracy and see it in action, it might enlighten them to the evils of Nazism. But because the Geneva Convention prohibited enemies from being subjected to propaganda, the Office of the Provost Marshal General had to tread carefully. Fortunately, it found a loophole in the Convention's Article 17. It stated, "So far as possible, belligerents shall encourage intellectual diversions and sports organized by prisoners of war." Since intellectual diversion was advocated, it remained up to the War Department to pick and choose the proper subjects and media. The representative of the War Department and the State Department determined "that if selected media for intellectual diversion were made available in the camps, the curiosity of the prisoners concerning the United States and its institutions would provide the means for their reeducation."[224] The program started on September 6, 1944, but it was top secret.

When Germany fell and victory was proclaimed in Europe in May 1945, many of the ordinary classes POWs had been taking were eliminated. Instead, the essentials—English, history, geography and others that stressed democracy—were emphasized. Books that were to be considered for class use, libraries and those for sale in the POW canteen all had to be read, analyzed and evaluated before they would be declared "suitable" for the POWs.[225] In addition, a national POW camp newspaper called Der Ruf was produced in 1945 by a group of nationally chosen POWs. Many Nebraska camps also created their own camp newsletters.

Although the Intellectual Diversion Program didn't eliminate Nazism in the camps, it did foster a new sense of intellectual discourse that challenged many POWs' prevailing views. Some POWs, like Wolfgang Dorschel in Fort Robinson, became passionate advocates for the project. Dorschel started a democracy discussion group that became popular with a large portion of the POW population at Fort Robinson. The Arbeitsgemeinschaft zur Pflege der Politischen Aufklärung (Working Association for Political Enlightenment) began with a group of twenty prisoners, nearly all progressive anti-Nazis, who for months met secretly in order to lay the groundwork for their democratic program. To belong to the society, an oath had to be taken—a permanent and unconditional break with National Socialism. By the end of July 1945, more than 90 percent of the prisoners at Fort Robinson had joined and had signed a contract to break with Nazism.[226]

After the war ended, it took some time for the prisoners to be returned to Germany. Many Nebraska farmers wanted them to stay longer to help fill the labor shortage until Nebraska soldiers returned. But the need for POWs to assist cleanup methods in Europe were far greater. By the end of July 1946, all POWs held in America had been shipped to Europe. Some went home to Germany, but more wound up in other POW camps throughout Europe for years before they were able to go home.

Most prisoners had a positive experience in Nebraska's POW camps. Indeed, many would return years later for reunions with former camp guards and American friends. Some, after returning to Germany after the war, immigrated to Nebraska and settled in areas where they'd formerly been prisoners. They became integral members of their communities as business owners, volunteers, residents and friends.[227]

Chapter 6

WAR PRODUCTION ON THE PLAINS

Even before the attack on Pearl Harbor, the U.S. government sought to shore up the nation's defenses by building new ammunition depots and defense manufacturing plants across the country. Nebraska's central location, isolated as it was from both coasts, offered the perfect spot for such industries. However, it took some time for Nebraska to be awarded defense contracts. Other Great Plains states, like Kansas and Oklahoma, welcomed war industries as early as December 1940. Nebraskans groused over their being ignored by the federal government for such industries. As early as November 1941, Senator George Norris received confirmation from Secretary of War Henry Stimson that Nebraska would be considered for ammunition depots.[228] The military chose Wahoo as a location for an ordnance plant, but the citizens of Hastings, Grand Island and Kearney lobbied to relocate it farther west into their area. Other squabbles over the few defense locations selected for Nebraska followed, and Norris grew fed up with Nebraskans. "If the Nebraska people are going to object every time a site is located, because it is not located in some other place, then we ought to…ask the government not to do anything in the way of national defense projects in the state of Nebraska."[229]

Despite Nebraskans' complaints, four ammunition and ordnance plants as well as one bomber plant were built in Nebraska: the Naval Ammunition Depot in Hastings, the Cornhusker Ordnance Plant in Grand Island, the Sioux Army Depot in Sidney, the Mead Ordnance Plant (aka the Nebraska Ordnance Plant) near Wahoo and the Glenn L. Martin Bomber Nebraska

Company in Omaha at Fort Crook. Many other factories in the state converted to war production. For example, the Scott-Omaha Tent and Awning Company in Omaha produced airplane hangars and tents for the military around the world, while Cushman Motorworks in Lincoln switched from making auto glides for civilian automobiles to almost exclusively producing bomb fuses. A windmill and farm implement manufacturing company in Beatrice, Dempster Mill Manufacturing, began making steel casings for 155mm shells. Some businesses found their products necessary to war work and simply stepped up production. The Petersen Manufacturing Company in DeWitt made the Vise-Grip wrench, and since it was an invaluable tool for building airplanes and ships, it found itself making thousands of them for war workers across the country.

The factories provided employment for not only Nebraskans but also others from around the country looking for work. Nebraska women flocked to the factories. Indeed, management placed want ads in newspapers specifically asking for women to apply, and they responded in droves so much so that they became known as WOWs (women ordnance workers).

The work was not without danger, however. Employees at ordnance factories worked with highly explosive and flammable materials, and accidents happened, some fatal. At the bomber plant, three separate accidents occurred with flying the B-26 and B-29 bombers, but no industrial accidents occurred.

Still, the work was "essential war work" and needed to be done to defeat the Axis. These ordnance plants contributed to the United States winning the war, and Nebraskans who worked there did so out of a combination of patriotism and high wages.

Significantly, these defense contracts offered a huge economic boom to Nebraska and the Great Plains overall, pulling the region out of the Great Depression. Unfortunately, not every area benefited equally. Some towns saw a loss of skilled workers as they flocked to areas where factories were located, while other towns had such an increase in population that housing shortages occurred. According to Douglas Hurt, "World War II...was merely an economic flash in the pan for the Great Plains."[230]

Cornhusker Ordnance Plant, Grand Island

Senator George Norris made an announcement on February 13, 1942, of the new ordnance plant to be built in Grand Island, saying that it would cost between $25 million and $28 million to build.[231] Part of the U.S. Army's Armament, Munitions and Chemical Command, the plant's purpose was to "load, assemble, and pack bombs of various sizes....It also produced auxiliary boosters as well as ammonium nitrate for the various admixtures of TNT loaded into bombs." The Q.O. Ordnance Corporation, a subsidiary of the Quaker Oats Company of Chicago, was in charge of operating the plant.[232] Construction started at the end of March 1942 on land five miles west of Grand Island. The plant would eventually encompass twenty square miles. Three bomb loading lines, the actual areas where ammunition production occurred, consisted of several different buildings. These included receiving and storing warehouses, bomb prep buildings, cooling bays, melt/pour and nose buildings and packing and shipping buildings.[233]

Administration buildings and other employee-focused buildings were also built. Load Line III poured the factory's first 1,000-pound bomb on November 11, 1942, and the other two lines went into production in December that same year. During the war, the plant produced 90-, 220- and 260-pound fragmentation bombs, and 1,000- and 2,000-pound demolition bombs.[234] Before shipping, bombs were painted with yellow rings on the nose to signify completion.[235]

Workers were paid sixty to seventy cents per hour, and at its peak, the plant employed more than 4,200.[236] This resulted in a housing shortage in Grand Island. The plant's newspaper, the *Coplanter*, published numerous complaints, leading the administration to build on-site dormitories: two for men, two for women and one for married couples. Those with children had to find other accommodations but were again helped by plant administrators. In addition, the plant hired physically disabled veterans and civilians as well as teenagers, although they had to be at least eighteen years of age.[237]

Women made up more than 40 percent of the workforce at the plant and earned the same amount as their male counterparts. Management even provided on-site childcare, a rather unusual practice at the time.[238] Ellamae Spencer Moseley, who began working at the plant when she was eighteen, became the face of women ordnance workers across America in 1944. The War Department featured her in an article and a series of photos showing a WOW's typical first day on the job at a war plant. Ellamae worked alongside her sister and felt "very patriotic" in her new role drilling holes in shells. During her time at the plant, her hair changed color and became bright auburn due to working with radioactive materials. This happened to several other workers as well.[239]

New women employees proceed through their first few days at the Cornhusker Ordnance Plant in Grand Island, Nebraska. 1944. U.S. War Department, Office of the Chief of Ordnance, Cornhusker Ordnance Plant, U.S. National Archives, Record Group 156, Records of the Office of the Chief of Ordnance, 1797–1988, Identifier 292125.

Ellamae Spencer Moseley signs in for a day of work at the Cornhusker Ordnance Plant in Grand Island, Nebraska. 1944. Ellamae began working at the plant at the age of eighteen. U.S. War Department, Office of the Chief of Ordnance, Cornhusker Ordnance Plant, U.S. National Archives, Record Group 156, Records of the Office of the Chief of Ordnance, 1797–1988, Identifier 292126.

Although accidents were rare, the plant suffered a tragic one on May 26, 1945. Building 10, the melt-pour building on Loan Line IV, suddenly exploded. The explosion could be felt in Grand Island and numerous nearby communities. Sixty years later, plant worker Elmer Uhrich recalled his memories of that day to the Grand Island Independent:

> I was in the ramp (near Building 6 on Line 3 about one mile away). It was warm that day and we had the ramp doors open. I was facing east (away from the explosion) when I felt the air pressure or concussion. Then came the boom, the noise. I spun around on my heels and looked out the door and I told the girls (employees in his department), "Line Four just blew up."...The roof (of Bldg. 10, Line 4) went up 1,000 feet in the air. It broke in two and came down in two chunks. There was no fire but there was so much dust you could not see much as the pieces came close to the ground. The steam, water, and air pipes were broken, spewing steam and water. You could not see anything for about 15 minutes. Later we saw that all that was left was a pile of rubble where the building had been.[240]

Nine people lost their lives that day. Unfortunately, the exact cause was never found, but lightning may have been a factor.

The plant quit production the day Japan surrendered, August 14, 1945. It was reopened during the Korean War from 1950 to 1957 and again during the Vietnam War from 1965 to 1973.

THE NEBRASKA ORDNANCE PLANT, MEAD

Near the small community of Mead in Saunders County, the Mead Ordnance Plant, also called the Nebraska Ordnance Plant, stretched over 17,250 acres. Because it was located close to Omaha and had a good railway system nearby, it was an ideal location. Senator George Norris was instrumental in bringing the plant to Nebraska, and the announcement came in October 1941. The contract was drawn up in December 1941, and construction began in early 1942, lasting for about nine months and employing nearly nine thousand workers. The estimated cost for constructing the plant was $25 million.[241] The plant was owned by the Department of Defense and operated by the National Defense Corporation, and Lieutenant Colonel Floyd L. Strawn was the commanding officer. Firestone Rubber Company eventually took over management.

Those whose land was confiscated by the government for the plant did not take kindly to being pushed off. A letter to the editor from one of the farmers, John Gustafson, was rather blistering. If his story is true, he had a reason to gripe, as he wasn't paid as much as the owners of the land across the road from his:

> I lived and owned a farm where the Nebraska Ordnance plant is now. It had been mine for 40 years. I had $10,000 worth of improvements on my farm, so did the farm across the road from mine. I got $145 an acre. The farm across the road belonged to a Lincoln insurance company. They got $200 an acre. Theirs had three large sloughs on it; my farm had none, and if there was any difference in land mine was the best. That's the naked truth about it. This is the way the government treats us farmers. I had three sons, and as soon as they had taken my farm they took all three of my sons for the service.[242]

Some farmers took it further and actually sued the federal government. There were 176 tracts of land acquired by the federal government for the Mead plant in 1941, and owners of 145 of these land tracts accepted the awards offered to them by the government. However, 31 owners appealed the process. The case finally went to trial in August 1944. During the trial, 5 claimants withdrew from the lawsuit by accepting settlements; a federal jury awarded additional funds to the other claimants as a "fair price."[243] Many of the farmhouses were used as office buildings.

With the influx of construction workers and employees, housing became an issue. Mead was far too small to handle the population explosion, and Wahoo, with a population of under five thousand people, also struggled. In May 1942, the FHA approved a housing project to build forty-six houses in Wahoo. Even a large section of Lincoln, located about forty-five miles away, was declared a critical housing location in March 1943, with about eighty homes to be built specifically to rent to employees at Mead.[244] Fremont was also a location where workers could live, and unfortunately, some landlords spiked the rents in August 1942, leading to a rent freeze by Charles Yost, the area rent director.[245]

Finding enough employees for Mead also became an issue, one that would plague it through most of the war. For example, in 1944, farm workers, who already faced labor shortages, were asked by J.R. Kinder, state director of the war manpower commission, to help. "This spirit of cooperation at home is playing a big part in our fighting forces' successes against the axis," Kinder said. "We are going to have to utilize every bit of available manpower. Last year farm workers, during the off season, were of great help in staffing essential industries. They proved to be efficient workers and I am sure they can be called upon to volunteer again this year."[246]

Despite these challenges, the Mead plant became a critical component of the war effort. It was a load, assembly and plant facility for explosive weapons with four individual bomb load lines. It produced bombs from ninety to twelve thousand pounds, projectiles, shells and mines. Other facilities included a landfill, an ammonium nitrate production plant, a bomb booster assembly plant, burning grounds, a proving range, analytical laboratories, a sewage treatment plant and storage igloos similar to those at the Sioux Ordnance Depot and the Naval Ammunition Depot at Hastings.[247] Guards were on duty at all times around the plant and even used horses instead of autos to help save on gas costs. A newspaper kept workers informed of activities. Women formed a large part of the workforce, as they had at the Cornhusker Ordnance Plant.

Working at the plant came with risks. The possibility of TNT poisoning was very real. The danger came from "inhaling granlar [sic] TNT," according to an article in the Omaha World-Herald. One worker from Mead, a Mrs. Frank Vrba of Wahoo, died at the plant hospital from such poisoning. Plant officials kept a steady eye on the situation. "We have consulting physicians as well as our own medical unit. The workers are given the closest of attention and are carefully watched."[248]

A feature in the Omaha Sunday World-Herald Magazine informed Nebraskans of how the plant worked. With accompanying pictures, the story told of the step-by-step bomb-making and filling process. Pellet presses were used on the booster line, then shaker machines sifted crystallized ammonium nitrate into safety containers for shipment to the bomb-loading lines. Bomb casings received a coat of olive drab paint before being loaded. Liquid TNT was poured into kettles and buckets. The TNT was then "puddled" to remove air spaces and cracks caused by cooling. Bombs were then filled in the loading stations, with the tail pour being the final pour of liquid TNT. Workers also had to break down the air bubbles. Once a bomb was filled, it was stenciled with pertinent data and prepared for shipment. Every day, a certain number of bombs was split in half for inspection.

The story also showed the necessary safety precautions at the plant. Each day, every worker had to go through a "shake down." Hat brims, pockets and trouser cuffs were examined, and anything that might cause a spark—pocket knives, mechanical pencils, combs, hairpins, matches or lighters—was confiscated and held until the worker ended his or her shift for the day. Safety wear included goggles, face shields, respirators and overalls. Women usually covered their hair with bandannas. Before they could put on their civilian clothes again, workers had to take showers to remove the dust from gunpowder, amatol scrap and TNT, all of which could be dangerous to the skin.[249]

Remarkably, unlike the other ammunition depots in Nebraska, Mead never had an explosive incident. By the time it stopped war production in August 1945, it had "a record of production estimated at 2,840,000 bombs ranging from 90-pounders to four-thousand pounders, an explosion poundage of 1,800,000,000 since September 10, 1942."[250]

After the war, the Nebraska Ordnance Plant stayed open but operated on a much smaller scale. It built ordnance for the Korean and Vietnam Wars. Some of the land was transferred to the University of Nebraska–Lincoln in 1962. Unfortunately, "during the late 1970s and early '80s, the university hauled hazardous waste to the site and buried it in trenches and a landfill, contributing to contamination already on the site from U.S. military activities."[251] The groundwater and soil contamination was also caused by the activities from the ordnance plant during the war. Cleanup is still ongoing today.

NAVAL AMMUNITION DEPOT, HASTINGS

Located about twenty-five miles south of Grand Island, Hastings was a medium-sized community in Adams County of about fifteen thousand people in 1940. But after the U.S. Naval Ammunition Depot was built, the town exploded in size, swelling to more than twenty-two thousand by 1944. Even though the increase in population led to its own set of challenges—racial tensions, housing shortages and rent gouging, to name a few—the depot itself churned out an incredible amount of ammunition for the U.S. Navy: a stunning 40 percent. It was the largest ammunition depot in the United States, covering 48,753 acres of land (seventy-six square miles).[252]

Senator George Norris announced the depot's contract on June 10, 1942, and in the next day's Nebraska State Journal, the editors wrote, "The midwest is to become the arsenal of America, just as America is the arsenal of the world."[253] Hastings was chosen for the project because of its location midway between both coasts, its proximity to the electrical power from the Tri-County project and its excellent railroad connections. Costs to build it were estimated at $45 million, and construction began immediately in July 1942.[254]

Unfortunately, most of the land was already being used as farm ground, and that meant several family farms suddenly became condemned. According to Walter L. Miller, farmers received notice via registered mail that the U.S. government needed their land, with orders to vacate in as little as two weeks or up to nine months, depending on the construction timetable. The Second War Powers Act of May 18, 1942, made the land grab possible. For some farmers who'd had the land for generations, the news was devastating. Lee Saathoff, an Adams County farmer, remembered his grandfather losing the farm at the age of fifty-eight. He'd paid $40,000 for the farm in 1914 and received only $16,119 from the government in 1943. "The only time I ever saw him cry was as he was leaving that farm."[255]

Construction lasted about eighteen months and included an influx of five thousand people for construction needs alone, straining the housing resources of Hastings. The few empty apartments and houses available were quickly snatched up, with some landlords increasing rent prices so much that U.S. Navy officials became involved. To alleviate the crowding, the U.S. Navy set up a trailer court in Hastings and also started construction on Spencer Park by building 840 concrete block apartments.[256]

The U.S. Navy had certain specifications for depot constructions, and the majority of them were for safety reasons and storage purposes:

The size and layout of the site established by Navy specifications required 700 bulk explosive vaults at twenty per square mile, over 1,000 ammunition bunkers, 65 factories, industrial headquarters area and hundreds of miscellaneous buildings. All structures used for explosives were strategically placed with huge 500-foot safety zones between them to avoid a chain reaction in case of an accidental explosion, and to keep the loss of life to a minimum. Nearly 300 miles of roads and 200 miles of railroad track connected all these structures. A security fence ran for 40 miles around the perimeter. All original county road mile intersections were blocked with railroad tie barriers thus allowing access at only 3 guarded entry gates into the facility.[257]

Such a huge establishment necessarily demanded a large workforce, as well as security by U.S. marines and the U.S. Coast Guard, along with

An aerial view of the Hastings Naval Ammunition Depot in the late 1940s. ACHS 142-12. Adams County Historical Society.

K-9 dogs, to protect against sabotage and keep the depot safe. The first contingent of U.S. marines came to the depot in December 1942. There were 7,584 civilians and 2,089 military personnel.

Potential employees filled out employment applications and took a physical at the hospital located at the depot. Once hired, they were photographed, fingerprinted and given an ID badge. They also had to undergo two days of instruction in military base regulations and were given the civilian worker manual. This handbook emphasized the need for security. "Never discuss with friends or strangers the progress of your work. Do not give out any details concerning your job on this Depot. Any such act will have serious consequences under the Espionage Act of 1917."[258]

Due to an employee shortage, more than 1,450 black sailors and 383 black civilians, men and women, also worked in labor or "ordnance battalions" at the depot. The arrival of these black families caused a surge of racism and discrimination in Hastings and the depot itself.[259] Lorena Smith, who lived in Hastings at the time, remembered, "We had not had black people [among us]. A lot of people did not like to see the black people around. They wouldn't even sit beside them on the bus....There was no reason for them not to like these people, but that's the way it was."[260] The black population in the Great Plains, particularly in the small towns of Nebraska, was not large, and thus, when they moved to predominantly white towns, issues arose.

According to historian R. Douglas Hurt, "It was not that they [Hastings residents] were not prejudiced; they were...the problem was that the white population of Hastings was unprepared to practice segregation on a grand scale. The town did not have separate recreational facilities and other establishments dedicated to serving blacks alone."[261] Black workers or service men and women were often turned away from restaurants, taverns and bowling alleys, as well as recreational facilities at the depot itself. They lived in subpar housing, and some Hastings homeowners even tried to keep them from living at the Pleasant Hills Trailer Camp northwest of Hastings (they were ultimately unsuccessful). However, grocery and merchandise stores served them without issue, as did movie theaters.[262]

But the discrimination and lack of recreational facilities eventually caused racial tensions to explode between whites and blacks at the depot. On June 10, 11 and 14, fights broke out at the barracks area, and by the evening of the fourteenth, things had escalated. A black sailor was put in the brig for intoxication by the Shore Patrol, and sixty other black sailors showed up to protest, leading to the detainment of five more men, although they were soon released. The navy launched an official investigation on June 20 and found that the "disturbances" were caused by "low morale encouraged by a 'weakened system of discipline,' a system that had been brewing for some time." In addition, the investigation found that "the commanding officer had lost the respect of the black enlisted men and that he was unable to enforce discipline." Thus, the commanding officer was replaced, and a new one took over on July 20. He made some changes, including shipping off those men who'd been involved in the disturbances and bringing in black women from Omaha to USO dances (a USO for black servicemen was opened at 624 West First Street in Hastings) for the black servicemen.[263]

In addition, a group of Sioux Native Americans from the South Dakota Pine Ridge Rosebud Reservation moved to Hastings. The Indian agent in Alliance asked several of the Native Americans working at the Alliance Airfield if they were interested in working at the Hastings Depot, and many accepted rather than go back to the reservation.[264] But once they arrived at the depot, they faced discrimination as well. R. Douglas Hurt wrote that "locals referred to them as 'braves' who were 'on the war path.' They lived

An unidentified worker at the Hastings Naval Ammunition Depot. Circa 1946. ACHS 143-34. Adams County Historical Society.

segregated and isolated lives in tents and congregated at the post office lobby, where as a 'federal people' they felt safe."[265]

As time went on, however, Hastings residents and depot employees learned to live and work together. Employees earned about seventy-four cents an hour, and like at other war plants around the country, women made up a large part of the workforce. The depot put out its own weekly newsletter, called the Powder Keg, and also had a baseball team that competed with Army Airfield teams Grand Island, Kearney and Fairmont, as well as the teams from Doane and Dana College. A racially integrated basketball team of black and white players also competed against nearby teams.

The depot officially opened on February 22, 1943, and on July 4, the first load of ammunition was ready to be delivered to the navy. Production continued until August 1945. The depot produced 40mm shells, rockets, 16in projectiles, bombs, mines, torpedoes and depth chargers. However, working with such dangerous materials was far from safe, and the depot suffered four fatal explosions, all in 1944. Twenty-one people were killed and hundreds injured.[266]

Black workers stand in line at the cafeteria mess hall at the Hastings Naval Ammunition Depot. There were separate dining areas for black and white service men and women. 1944. Hastings, Nebraska. U.S. National Archives, Department of Defense, Department of the Navy, 9th Naval District, Office of the Commandant, Identifier 283488.

Following the end of World War II, ammunition was sent back to the depot to be disassembled. While some was stored in anticipation of the next war, others were safely destroyed. The depot itself, with reduced employees, stayed open until 1949, when it was put on standby. Production started again with the Korean War in 1950 and triggered a $20 million expansion of the depot. In 1959, the 625th Bomb Scoring Unit of the U.S. Air Force was based at the depot. The U.S. Marine Corps and the U.S. Navy eventually left in 1966, and the depot provided housing for military families of the U.S. Air Force. Finally, in 1966, the depot was completely decommissioned. The federal government did not return to the farmers any of the land it had taken to build the depot.[267]

Sioux Army Depot, Sidney

In March 1942, citizens of the sparsely populated Panhandle county of Cheyenne learned that Sidney would become home to a new ordnance depot. Some met the news with skepticism and worry, while others rejoiced at the thought of the area getting a much-needed injection of money to help grow the community.

As it turns out, there would be winners and losers. Once again, farmers found themselves kicked off their land to make way for war construction. Thirty-five farm families sold their land to the government ostensibly at a fair price and never received those nineteen thousand acres back. (Instead, after the depot was decommissioned in the late 1960s, some other farmers pooled their money and bought back some of the land.) But the town of Sidney went from a population of 3,300 to more than 10,000 during the construction phase, and when the base was completed, permanent workers moved into the area.[268] The depot created an economic boom for the town, but it wasn't without its drawbacks.

The depot's site, located twelve miles northwest of Sidney, had originally been rejected as an ammunition storage facility site in 1941 because planners believed it was not suited to storing lethal gas. However, it was later deemed appropriate due to its dry climate and isolation and because it "provided a proper geographic and strategic balance of ammunition stocks."[269] The U.S. Army Engineers wasted no time in beginning construction on the site and was allotted eight months to complete the project. The depot's mission was described as follows: "[T]he receipt, storage, and issue of Army ammunition, ammunition components, and general supplies."[270]

With a population of 3,300, Sidney wasn't prepared for the influx of people. In June 1942, an article in the Omaha World-Herald discussed how the town was about to "burst its seams." Contractors called for "thousands of laborers," which soon led to a housing shortage. Trailer camps and temporary barracks sprang up to address the shortage. Some people also lived in nearby towns. Feeding all those workers also created a problem, with "cafés crowded night and day." In response, the government decided to build a mess hall at the construction site to try to ease the burden on the town itself. Since the town only employed three police officers, they added five more to their staff, and the county sheriff also hired an additional deputy. However, Sidney citizens appeared to enjoy the excitement: "After a decade of farm depression the sudden unprecedented activity seems to have caught the public fancy."[271]

However, some unscrupulous people took advantage of the situation by increasing rent prices. This caused tension between the army and the city of Sidney so much so that the commanding general of the U.S. Army 7th Corps Area issued a stern warning in the Sidney Telegraph. Because of "rent profiteers" and "price hijackers," he declared that instead of relying on the town of Sidney for the army's needs, the army itself would supply it—building barracks, stores, movie theaters and all other necessities. The newspaper editors weren't shy in their response to the army, castigating those Sidney residents for causing problems. "This newspaper isn't going to sit here and watch a handful of slackers put the brand on all the rest of us," they stated.[272] The warnings worked.

On July 31, Jack Lowe, an Associated Press correspondent and Sidney journalist, wrote, "There's just one way to describe Sidney these days… the town has gone nuts."[273] The town had swelled to ten thousand, nearly triple the original population, but somehow people muddled through and made it work. A federal housing project in mid-1942 also helped alleviate the overcrowding.

Construction proceeded rapidly on the depot, which comprised four main areas: administrative (administrative building, dispensary, fire and guard house, mess hall, barracks, gate guard house, telephone exchange and other buildings), utilities (carpenter shop, lumber storage yard, machine shop, garages, storehouses, locomotive house, sewage plants, fuel and water tanks, power generator plant and more), combat equipment storage area (warehouses and loading platforms) and the magazine area (aboveground magazines, igloos, inspectors' workshops, bundle ammunition packing buildings, shipping buildings and so on). Rail facilities had two classification yards and two inspection pits. Each of the major railroads, Burlington and Union Pacific, had lines here, and the railroad was used to ship ammunition to its destination.[274]

By August 1942, the depot wasn't quite finished, but enough construction had been completed to begin hiring skilled workers and laborers. Almost immediately, the army had difficulty hiring enough workers. Sidney was a small community, and the majority of people were farmers or worked in agricultural-based careers. Therefore, the army broadened its search, recruiting workers from western and northwestern Nebraska towns. However, this labor force consisted strictly of men. It wasn't until November 27 that women were hired as crate assemblers and then, on December 1, as guards.[275] A manpower shortage would continue to plague the depot throughout its existence for several reasons. Wage competition was perhaps the biggest. The Hastings Naval Depot paid seventy-five cents an hour for a fifty-six-hour workweek, while the Sioux Depot paid sixty and sixty-five cents an hour for a forty-eight-hour workweek. Gas rationing also made recruitment difficult, as the population density in western Nebraska was far less than in eastern Nebraska, requiring people to travel farther to work.[276]

Operations officially began in December 1942 and proceeded steadily. The labor shortage eventually led the War Manpower Commission to declare the depot a "critical area" in August 1943, after which troops from Wyoming were brought to Sidney for training. The depot also created a school to help women learn how to drive forklifts and trucks.[277]

But in 1944, a new source of labor helped alleviate the shortage: Italian prisoners of war. Captured during the North African campaign, the Italians had been held in Scottsbluff since June 1943. Since Italy's surrender in September 1943, the Italians were technically no longer prisoners, but because they could not yet return home and were needed to alleviate the labor shortage, they could volunteer to work at military-related installations. Several hundred were sent to the Sioux Army Depot in January 1944 and, according to an article, seemed "anxious to work." With ages ranging from seventeen to fifty-two, they were employed as carpenters, cooks, mechanics, laborers, hospital attendants and even engineers, and they had their own barracks. Apparently, the Italians acquired quite a few animal companions, as the article stated that "pets and dogs and cats are numerous in the prisoners' quarters."[278] When the Italians left in September 1945, German prisoners of war were brought in to help.

The Italians and Germans were not the only ones to help bridge the labor gap. In September 1944, the War Department announced that Japanese American internees from camps around the country would be working at the Sioux Depot as well as another ordnance depot in Utah. According to the official announcement, the internees would be there on "their own free will" and would be under civil service regulations. In addition, they would "enjoy equal rights with the other workers."[279] The official history of the depot stated that these workers and their families "became an indispensable part of the community and proved to be highly valuable employees."[280]

After the war ended, the Sioux Depot continued operations as overseas shipments of ordnance came in, necessitating storage. The depot stayed in operation through the Korean War and up until 1967. The buildings at the depot were then used at the new Western Nebraska Technical School and eventually became a part of Western Nebraska Community College.

Today, one can still see the ammunition igloos that dot the countryside near Sidney. Called Corbetta-type igloos, their construction "consisted of steel and concrete, which was water-proofed and earth covered. Special seed was sown over and between all the igloos. Each one was equipped with steel doors and ventilators." About 802 igloos were constructed.[281]

The Sioux Depot played an important role in western Nebraska during the war, forever altering the landscape and challenging the citizens of Sidney and other, smaller communities nearby to adapt to a wartime footing. In this they succeeded.

Glenn L. Martin–Nebraska Company, Fort Crook, Omaha

Based in Baltimore, the Glenn L. Martin Company was a powerhouse of war production during World War II. But in 1940, its Baltimore plant wasn't large enough to produce bombers needed for the U.S. Army Air Forces and the Lend-Lease program to Great Britain.[282] The government approved plans in December 1940 to build an assembly plant and modification center for the Martin B-26 medium bombers at Fort Crook (Omaha), Nebraska. Fort Crook, established in 1888, had become an induction center and a maintenance/supply depot after the attack on Pearl Harbor. Now, however, it would fulfill a crucial role in the war against the Axis.

The contract for the bomber plant signed with Omaha-based Condon and Peter Kiewit Company and Lincoln-based Woods Brothers totaled nearly $8 million.[283] Construction began in early 1941, and when it finished in late 1941, there was about 1.2 million square feet of total floor space, nearly equal to five football fields.[284] Production work began in the plant on December 15, 1941, and was "spasmodic" up until July of that year owing to start-up necessities like installing machines, setting up departments and other procedures. But the first B-26C built at the Fort Crook plant rolled off the assembly line and was accepted by the U.S. Army Air Forces in August 1942, and production steadily increased month by month, hitting its stride in April 1943.[285]

It's important to note that the factory did not build every single part of the B-26. Instead, as George A. Larson wrote, "The assembly of one B-26 required 25,000 manufactured parts, not counting engines and instruments. Approximately fifty percent of the work required to build the B-26 was done at the Omaha site."[286] The plant manufactured sheet metal–detailed parts, machined parts, motor mounts and empennage (tail assembly) and aileron surfaces, among others. Subcontractors manufactured other parts, including wings, landing gear and body sections.[287]

The plant employed thousands of people from Nebraska, nearby states and across the country. At its height (January 1945), well over thirteen thousand people worked at the bomber plant. If they passed the physical examination, each potential employee would then take a battery of tests, either clerical (typing, transcription, dictation and so on) or factory (mechanical aptitude and comprehension), as well as personality tests. Test scores were compiled and then attached to the applicant's credentials to be used at the final interview.[288] Jobs included far more than just working on the factory floor. Writers, typists, accountants, tailors, photographers, cooks, chauffeurs and more were needed to keep the factory running smoothly. In November 1944, women made up more than 40 percent of the workers.[289]

Once hired, employees had their photos taken for their work badges, they were fingerprinted and then they were given a tour of the factory—which undoubtedly impressed many. During the tour, they were warned to keep details about the assembly and manufacturing of the plant confidential. The tour guide said, "Never repeat any information which you have not seen printed already for the Public."[290] Because most of the plant's employees had never worked in a plane factory before, the plant provided training courses. These courses lasted an average of two weeks and were conducted entirely during the employee's company time, at no cost to the employee. Each position had a detailed written description of the duties involved, a job classification and a pay grade.

The plant functioned as a small town. Multiple cafeterias, a hotel, a library, recreation and transportation facilities, a post office and more composed the factory grounds. With the influx of workers not only to the bomber plant but also to the various other war industries located in Omaha, a housing shortage cropped up. The local war-housing authority stepped up to address the problem, and although it took time, by December 1944, 369 new homes had been built in Omaha.[291]

On April 29, 1943, President Roosevelt paid a visit to the plant along with Governor Dwight Griswold, General Manager G.T. Willey and Glenn Martin. Factory employees were ecstatic at the visit, stopping work to greet him as his car drove through the plant:

Everywhere the president went, employees abandoned their tools, their presses, punches, drills, rollers and shears, and the spic and span plant was quietexceptforapplauseandcheers....Thechiefexecutivehimselfwas sointerestedthathekeptacontinualstreamof questionsgoingatMartin, Willey and the governor.[292]

However, the factory was about to switch gears. The B-26 was soon to be replaced by a far superior plane: the B-29 Boeing Superfortress. Boeing described the B-29 as follows:

Oneof themosttechnologicallyadvancedairplanesof WorldWar2,the B-29hadmanynewfeatures,includinggunsthatcouldbefiredbyremote control.Twocrewareas,foreandaft,werepressurizedandconnectedby alongtubeoverthebombbays,allowingcrewmemberstocrawlbetween them.Thetailgunnerhadaseparatepressurizedareathatcouldonlybe enteredorleftataltitudesthatdidnotrequirepressurization.TheB-29 wasalsotheworld'sheaviestproductionplanebecauseof increasesin range, bomb load and defensive requirements.[293]

Aerial view of the Martin Bomber Plant looking southeast, with Fort Crook at the right. Wing Historian's Office (WHO), circa 1945, Offutt Air Force Base, Glenn L. Martin–Nebraska Bomber Plant, Building D, Peacekeeper Drive, Bellevue, Sarpy County, Nebraska. Library of Congress, Identifier HAER NE-9-R-21.

After making the necessary modifications to the factory, including building a new $2 million expansion, production on the B-29s began in April 1944 and continued until after the war ended. One of those B-29 bombers would make history.

The plant produced fifteen "Silverplate" B-29s, which were specially modified to carry atomic bombs. Based on specifications from Colonel Paul Tibbets Jr. of the 509th Composite Group (a U.S. Army Air Forces unit tasked with carrying out the atomic bombings), the planes had all their armor plating and guns stripped except for the tail gunner position, which made the aircraft seven thousand pounds lighter. Tibbets visited the bomber plant on May 9, 1945, and, with the help of a few factory foremen, picked out the plane (simply labeled "82") that would drop the atomic bomb, nicknamed "Little Boy," on Hiroshima on August 6, 1945. Tibbets named the plane Enola Gay after his mother. The plane would fly as the weather plane during the second bombing, this time of Nagasaki, three days later on August 9, 1945. Another B-29 "Silverplate" plane

Detail view of the main assembly level looking northeast at the B-26 final production line showing the integrity of the "Bomb-Proof" building after the crash of a B-25 on September 22, 1943. WHO, 1943—Offutt Air Force Base, Glenn L. Martin–Nebraska Bomber Plant, Building D, Peacekeeper Drive, Bellevue, Sarpy County, Nebraska. Library of Congress, Identifier HAER NE-9-R-26.

Colonel Paul W. Tibbets Jr., pilot of the Enola Gay, the plane that dropped the atomic bomb on Hiroshima, waves from his cockpit before the takeoff. August 6, 1945. U.S. Army Air Forces. U.S. National Archives, Record Group 208, Records of the Office of War Information, 1926–1951, Identifier 535.

built at the Martin Bomber Plant, Bockscar, carried the Nagasaki bomb, nicknamed "Fat Man."[294]

Two fatal air crashes occurred at the Martin Bomber Plant during the war. The first happened on May 25, 1942, with a B-26A Marauder plane. Two test pilots, Carl W. Hartley and Henry K. Meyers, were testing a plane when the hatch cover over the pilot's compartment fell from the plane during its two-thousand-foot climb; the hatch cover then hit the vertical stabilizer. "The impact tore away the top portion of the stabilizer along with the entire rudder attached to it as the plane continued its upward momentum." Unfortunately, the pilots were unable to control the plane, and they came "nearly straight down in a vertical dive." The impact instantly killed the two pilots. After the investigation was completed, investigators discovered that the securing mechanism for the hatch needed to be properly secured, and in the future, a red warning tag was attached onto the hatch cover labeled "Inspect Latch Pins for Security." Although investigators never determined if Hartley's hatch had been properly secured, installing this safety feature most certainly saved other lives during the war.[295]

The second crash, on September 22, 1943, claimed the lives of Martin civilian employees as well as the military test pilot and cost thousands of dollars in damage to the main Martin assembly building. First Lieutenant E.D. Walborn piloted the B-25D plane, while civilian gunner Thomas P. Zinkevich was expected to test-fire the newly installed guns. The plane's engineer, Elmer W. Murphy, and James J. Leach, a Martin inspector, planned to check various aspects of the plane during the flight. However, while they were taxiing down the runway, smoke appeared from the left exhaust but briefly stopped when the plane became airborne. But soon smoke poured from the exhaust. Walborn shut down the engine and began circling the field to land. Unfortunately, on the final approach, the left wing dropped just as the plane was directly over the main Martin assembly building. In his book Nebraska's Fatal Air Crashes of World War II, author Jerry Penry explained what happened next:

> The bomber tore through the steel girders and immediately caught fire as workers still inside the building scrambled to get out of the way. Flames being fed by the ruptured fuel tanks shot upward through the roof of the plant as the plane remained temporarily hung up in the girders. Gasoline also leaked out of the plane onto the wooden block floor which threatened to spread and consume the engine….As the fire continued to consume the plane, the grip of the girders loosened, and the plane fell to the floor. The crashing

planestruckanewB-26Cthatwasinthefinalstagesof construction. Theforceoftheimpactcompletelydestroyedbothplanes....Sincetheplane hadbeenfullyloadedwithammunitionfortestfiringatthegunneryrange, the .50 caliber shells began exploding in the fire.[296]

Walborn was critically injured and later died at the hospital. Murphy and Leach were killed instantly. Zinkevich survived. The investigation later determined that the articulating rods of cylinders nos. 6, 8 and 10 in the left engine were broken, leading to engine failure. The damage to the building was estimated around $25,000.[297]

Production at the plant stopped in September 1945, and the final employees left in April 1946. The plant became a storage facility for a time, and then Fort Crook was transferred to the U.S. Air Force in 1948, becoming Offut Air Force Base.[298]

Chapter 7

THE NORTH PLATTE CANTEEN

t's been called a miracle, and in many ways, it was. The North Platte Canteen greeted soldiers going to war and those coming back from it, providing a place of warmth and hospitality in the midst of a world gone mad. Decades later, soldiers remembered their time at the canteen, and letters and thank-you notes poured into North Platte long after the canteen closed. The hard work, sacrifice and dedication of Nebraskans in North Platte and surrounding areas only solidified some of the slogans used to describe Nebraska throughout the years, namely "Nebraska, the Good Life" and "Nebraska Nice." The canteen has inspired books, both fiction and nonfiction, as well as documentaries, feature stories on national news networks like NPR and CBS This Morning, online exhibits and blog posts on the National World War II Museum website and the U.S. National Archives website, a plethora of articles and even plays and musicals.

In short, the story of the canteen remains popular largely not only because it made a huge impression on the public imagination during and after World War II but also because the soldiers who were guests there, if only for a brief moment, fondly remembered Nebraskans' generosity and kindness for years to come.

HUMBLE BEGINNINGS

Ten days after the bombing of Pearl Harbor, North Platte residents heard that the Nebraska National Guard would be passing through the town en route to the West Coast. Family and friends decided to gather at the Union Pacific train station to deliver good wishes as well as food and cigarettes for the troops. Unfortunately, when the train arrived, it carried a National Guard unit from Kansas. Instead of taking their offerings home, the group decided to shower the Kansas troops with gratitude and goodies. This simple act sparked an idea with twenty-six-year-old Rae Wilson, whose brother was the commander of the local National Guard unit. Wouldn't it be a wonderful idea to greet all troop trains the way they'd greeted the Kansas National Guard?

Wilson wrote a letter to the North Platte Daily Bulletin on December 18, 1941, encouraging the citizens of North Platte to start a canteen and offered to volunteer her time. "To see the spirits and the high morale among those soldiers should certainly put some of us on our feet and make us realize we are really at war," she wrote. "We should help keep this soldier morale at its highest peak. We should do our part." Wilson ended with, "I say get back of our sons and other mothers' sons 100 percent. Let's do something and do it in a hurry! We can help this way when we can't help any other way."[299]

Volunteers at the North Platte Canteen display some of the baked goods available for service men and women. Lincoln County Historical Museum, North Platte, Nebraska.

Wilson immediately got to work. She contacted "friends, businessmen and civic leaders" in North Platte about her idea. The response was immediate, and by December 25, 1941, a mere seven days after Wilson's letter to the editor, the canteen officially opened. Originally, canteen volunteers prepared meals in the nearby Cody Hotel and stored baked goods in a maintenance shed near the depot; then they would meet the trains. Obviously, this wouldn't work in the long term, so Wilson personally approached the president of Union Pacific Railroad, W.F. Jeffers, a North Platte native, about using the passenger station along Front Street and the UP tracks. It had closed in 1940, but it featured a large public lunchroom that would be perfect for use as a canteen. Jeffers eagerly agreed to let her use the lunchroom, and by January 1, 1942, the canteen volunteers had moved in. In addition, for the duration of the canteen's existence, Jeffers also provided heat, water, cups and napkins. He even bought a dishwashing machine and hired UP employees to do the janitorial work. In addition, Jeffers saw to it that UP publicized the canteen, printing up thousands of postcards and brochures and having UP conductors go through the troop trains to alert service members to the stop they'd be making at North Platte.[300]

MAKING IT WORK

The first month the canteen was in operation, it served more than twenty-six thousand soldiers.[301] It was an amazing accomplishment, made all the more special because it had no longer become just a North Platte–led endeavor but rather a statewide and nationwide one. As the canteen continued, letters poured in from soldiers across the nation as well as other Americans. Numerous community newspapers around the nation were publishing articles about the canteen, and people began to send in packages of cigarettes and playing cards, magazines, soap and other nonperishable items.[302]

However, Rae Wilson and other canteen volunteers knew that it would take incredible tenacity to keep the canteen going, especially in light of ration restrictions. As Bob Greene wrote, "The willingness of the Canteen volunteers to simply give away food was even more striking in light of the specific restrictions placed on American families by the government during the war years. It wasn't just the selflessness of the volunteers, although that was impressive enough; it was their selflessness in the face of personal deprivation."[303]

Here's just one example of the food served at the canteen, provided by volunteer Daisy C. Hinman in 1944:

Each day, from one to five thousand men in uniform hurry through the big door for a ten-minute pause on their journey into the unknown. They see long tables laden with good things to eat: great platters of sandwiches, pickles, hard-boiled eggs, cookies, doughnuts, cake and coffee; milk too, and on hot days, iced tea, pop, sometimes ice cream cones. From the farm homes come fried chicken and hundreds of pies. The mothers, wives and sweethearts of men already fighting, and who serve them so gladly, urge them to take all they want. Always there are birthday cakes, beautifully decorated, and enough so that every boy with a birthday that week can have his own cake. Then everybody sings with a will. "Happy birthday to you!!" He leaves not only with his cake but often with tears in his eyes, feeling that this world is a wonderful place after all. One of our workers has baked an angel-food birthday cake every Saturday for the past two years, and considers it a privilege.[304]

As discussed in the first chapter on rationing, sugar was one of the first items to be restricted and continued until the war was over. How, then, was it possible to make all those cakes and goodies for the soldiers? The canteen was run like a business, with "elected officers, chairmen for all departments, a board of management, a grievance committee, and an accredited accountant,"[305] and they took their mission seriously. Mrs. I.C. Self was the logistical officer for the canteen and stayed on top of its supplies. When it would run low on items such as sugar, it usually placed articles in local newspaper asking for donations of supplies and ration coupons, and businesses and Nebraskans would respond. However, after learning a hard lesson in February 1943 when supplies ran short, Mrs. Self became "quite astute about rationing the supplies that were funneling their way through the Canteen, always being diligent to squirrel away whatever could be stockpiled."[306] Daily operating costs were about $125. One month in 1945, the canteen organizers counted to see how much food was distributed. Their totals were 40,161 cookies; 30,679 hard-boiled eggs; 6,547 doughnuts; 6,939 cup, loaf and birthday cakes; 2,845 pounds of sandwich meat; and 12 dozen different items in similar proportions.[307] It was an impressive accomplishment.

Service organizations, churches and other groups stepped up to the plate, and thus a Canteen Club was started to "honor and recognize" those who volunteered and contributed to the canteen. Some of them included the American Legion Auxiliary of Sidney, the Platte Valley Club, the Veterans of Foreign Wars, the North Platte Episcopal Church, the American Legion Auxiliary, the North Platte Chamber of Commerce and many more. Groups from small towns such as Arcadia, North Loop and even Huxton, Colorado, drove to the canteen with carloads full of supplies like meat, bread, butter, donuts, oranges, milk, candy bars, magazines and much more. With the help of these groups and other individuals, the canteen was able to operate for the duration of the war. In addition to supplies, monetary donations were also accepted on site, with numerous soldiers contributing to the donation jar.[308]

Funds were also raised in other ways. Perhaps one of the most well-known fundraisers was a young boy named Gene Slattery from Big Springs, Nebraska. After hearing tales about the canteen and how it needed money to operate, the ten-year-old decided to sell some of his goats, "which were by way of becoming a nuisance," and donated the money to the canteen in

A North Platte Canteen volunteer gives a U.S. sailor a birthday cake. Lincoln County Historical Museum, North Platte, Nebraska.

1943.[309] Then, while in North Platte for Future Farmers of America's annual Chicken Day, he auctioned off his chickens and donated the profits. But in an astonishing move, he also auctioned off the shirt from his back, earning more than $36. The winning bidder returned Slattery's shirt to him so that he could continue to fundraise, and that's exactly what the young man did. He began to travel to auctions throughout western Nebraska to auction off his shirt—about eighteen times—and by the war's end, he'd raised more than $2,000 for the canteen.[310] He even wrote a letter to President Roosevelt and "asked him to join the canteen club which makes monthly donations." He received a note in response from the president's private secretary saying that, unfortunately, the chief executive couldn't join more organizations but praised Gene for his hard work. Enclosed with the letter was a $5 bill, which Slattery made sure to give to the canteen.[311]

Because the canteen became such a huge success, it had the unfortunate consequence of making founder Rae Wilson unable to continue at the helm due to the ill effects on her health. Helen Christ then took over the responsibilities for the duration.

SERVING THE SOLDIERS

From that first stop of National Guardsmen in December 1941 through April 1, 1946, the canteen served about 6 million servicemen.[312] It was a monumental feat. Up to twenty-four trains stopped at the canteen on any given day. But even though the canteen personnel and volunteers felt immense pride in contributing to the war effort by doing all they could to help the service men and women feel their warmth and hospitality, it was the service men and women themselves who really benefited the most. In his book Once Upon a Town, Bob Greene shared numerous stories from soldiers he spoke with who had stopped at the canteen. More than fifty years later, the canteen still held a special place in their hearts, and with good reason.

As Matthew Norton discussed in his thesis on the North Platte Canteen, soldiers often had wearying train journeys with broken heaters during the winter and stifling train carriages during the summer. When stopping at stations, food and other items were often expensive, and troops usually had to stay onboard. It did little to help morale. But when they pulled into North Platte, they were introduced to an entirely new experience and shown the patriotic spirit and gratefulness of the Americans for whom they were fighting. Here they were treated like kings and queens. Here, for ten or fifteen minutes, they gathered around a piano and sang songs, ate birthday cakes and sandwiches, drank hot coffee, chatted with the locals, flirted with pretty girls and, in some instances, met future spouses.

One soldier, who stopped at the canteen twice, wrote a glowing letter to Reader's Digest. Then stationed in the Pacific, Lieutenant Irving Bennett wrote:

> I've seen railroad canteens, but this one had them beat. There must have been one hundred townspeople in the room—the men with sleeves rolled, the women in aprons, the girls in pretty dresses.... There were mountains of sandwiches, of cakes, of doughnuts, of candy; there were gallons of coffee and cases of milk; tables bulged with books and magazines. The heart-warming anxious smiles of the people told us better than any sign that it was "free."... This town must repeat this scene many times a day. I wish that they could know that there are many of us who remember well our 10-minute stop at North Platte, Neb. To us this memory will grow brighter and be as a beacon light on the road home. We thank God for these good people of a good land who bring a touch of humanity and everlasting kindness into the lives of boys making the long trip from home.[313]

This effusive praise was echoed in hundreds of other letters as well, proving how much of a difference the canteen made in the lives of these soldiers. The canteen volunteers also did not discriminate based on race. Even though the U.S. military was segregated, it didn't matter to those at the canteen. They served black soldiers just as warmly as they did other races. One famous picture shows a group of canteen volunteers serving a birthday cake to a black serviceman.

Other Allied soldiers also passed through the canteen. "One of the first groups of Allied personnel to travel through North Platte came in the form of thirty members of the Russian Red Army, survivors of a steamer ship that sunk in the Atlantic," Norton wrote in Catering to the Troops. "They spoke little English but they quickly realized the generosity behind the complimentary food and beverage for which they were extremely grateful." Three officers from Brazil also experienced the hospitality at the canteen. "Much like the Russian soldiers, the Brazilian officers felt surprised and awestruck that such hospitality was extended to soldiers outside of the United States armed forces."[314] Soldiers from England, China, France, the Netherlands and French Morocco also passed through the canteen doors. But for the volunteers, it didn't matter where these service men and women called home—they welcomed them and showed them Nebraska hospitality.

Volunteers at the North Platte Canteen present a birthday cake to a black U.S. Army soldier. Even though the U.S. Army was segregated, the volunteers did not discriminate on the basis of race, but rather served all equally. Lincoln County Historical Museum, North Platte, Nebraska.

The canteen's reputation spread. In December 1943, the canteen was awarded the War Department's Meritorious Wartime Service Award. National magazines and newspapers including Liberty magazine, the military's magazine; Stars and Stripes; National Geographic; and even the New York Times featured stories on the canteen. The U.S. Army sent a ten-man team to film the canteen in August 1945, and the film is currently in the U.S. National Archives (you can watch the video on its YouTube channel).

AFTER THE WAR

Long after the war ended in August 1945, the canteen stayed open, determined to welcome home as many troops as possible. When, in late 1945, Mrs. Helen Christ from the canteen expressed concern that Union

Pacific Railroad would need to close the canteen to make room for other business, UP president William M. Jeffers reassured her that such a thing would not happen. "Most certainly, it is my view that the canteen should be continued until the big movement of returning servicemen is over. You women have done a great job in the North Platte canteen and it would be too bad to have that record marred by an untimely closing."[315]

For Christmas that year, the canteen put on a spectacular celebration. Due to a travel snarl, numerous men and women in the military were unable to be home for Christmas, and between seven and eight thousand ended up at the canteen. A glittering Christmas tree and gifts for all, plus plenty of food, greeted the travel-weary troops. Some local servicemen and their wives and families even gave up their personal Christmas celebrations to be at the canteen. It seemed like the canteen had pulled off a Christmas miracle.[316]

As 1946 rolled in, all types of donations continued to pour into the canteen, as well as thank-you letters from all across the nation. But finally, with fewer troop trains coming through, the canteen committee decided to close its doors on April 1, 1946. Unfortunately, the railroad demolished the depot in 1973, although there is a small memorial to the canteen located nearby.

During the five years the canteen was open, about fifty-five thousand volunteers from 125 different towns had helped keep the canteen running. The canteen volunteers and those who sent donations exemplified the spirit of the day, where contributing to the war effort was not just an individual effort but a community one. While other canteens operated in different parts of the nation, perhaps none is remembered as fondly as the one in North Platte. Letters continued to arrive in North Platte decades after the canteen closed, and when veterans were later interviewed for various documentaries or books, they became emotional over the memory of their brief stop at the canteen.

Rae Wilson's small idea bloomed into a full-fledged national story, touching the hearts of millions of Americans during a time of war and filling them with hope that good did indeed triumph over evil.

Chapter 8

THE USO

Nebraska Women Serve the War Effort

World War II forever changed the landscape of the American workforce. With many men off fighting, the need for employees skyrocketed, and women answered the call in every industry. They drove taxis; worked in defense plants; cleaned train engines; worked as mechanics, bank tellers and managers; enlisted in the military; trained as nurses and more. For many women, this was their first job outside the home and provided a sense of independence, satisfaction and additional income. But it was also their way to contribute to the war effort and show their patriotism.

Nebraska women were no different, and they filled all of these positions vacated by men or worked in newly created jobs. With agriculture being Nebraska's main economic industry, many women worked on farms or ranches, although some found it more beneficial to find jobs in towns or nearby war plants. In addition to taking advantage of employment opportunities, women were also a driving force behind many volunteer organizations. Some women did both—working outside the home and volunteering. Others dedicated their time to volunteer efforts and fulfilled the traditional gender role of being a housewife. Nevertheless, they served on committees for the local USOs, volunteered with the Red Cross, donated books to send to the military and formed other groups that directly interacted with the troops. No matter what role they took, women were broadening their horizons and gaining skills for a postwar world.

In 1942, a book called Calling All Women: The American Women's Guide to Voluntary Service by Keith Ayling profiled several service organizations and helped women figure out where they could best serve the war effort, from civilian defense to the Red Cross to factory jobs. However, he did not believe that volunteer or defense work should take precedence over taking care of children: "[H]ome life must be maintained....I could not see that any woman's war work could justify neglect of the home. After all, why did the U.S.A. make its early draft laws so that the married men should not be taken into the armed forces? Simply because in the American way of living there is a deep-rooted respect for, and healthy desire to preserve the home."[317] In fact, Ayling was rather emphatic on the subject: "I can think of no greater tragedy than the American woman dumping her children in some nursery school and hurling herself willy-nilly into voluntary work at the expense of home and family."[318] This was the typical belief during this time, and indeed, the debate continues to rage on in current discourse. But Ayling still encouraged those women who stayed home to take care of the children to put their skills to use for the war effort wherever possible, whether it was sewing at home or canvassing the neighborhood for war bond funds.

Although service activities fit more easily into the traditional woman's role, they were anything but unimportant. Rather than driving a jeep or answering phones at a military base, these women put their domestic skills to use and thus weren't viewed through the same lens as those who volunteered for military service or who worked in industrial jobs. In essence, as Emily Yellin wrote, "These women were also less threatening to the status quo than their military counterparts, though they discovered a similar kind of satisfaction in using their skills and talents in public life."[319] There was not the usual discrimination and sexism within these activities as there was working a "man's job." But women handled these duties with aplomb and grace, running these organizations as efficiently as any business. One of the most popular organizations women participated in throughout the state of Nebraska was the USO.

In response to a request from President Franklin D. Roosevelt to provide morale, support and activities for U.S. military personnel, Mary Ingraham, a woman from Brooklyn, New York, started the USO in 1941. Six civilian organizations—the Salvation Army, Young Men's Christian Association (YMCA), Young Women's Christian Association (YWCA), National Catholic Community Service, National Travelers Aid Association and the National Jewish Welfare Board—all banded together to form the USO. While the government would provide funds for the buildings (from the National War Fund), operational expenses had to be raised through private funds.

Soon, USO centers opened around the world to fulfill the organization's motto of a "Home Away from Home" for the troops. The centers offered recreational activities, including live shows, movies, dances and other entertainment. Coffee and donuts were usually present, and in some centers, like Union Station in Omaha, there were quiet spots where servicemen could write letters. Hollywood celebrities became intrinsically entwined with the USO, performing at shows in the United States and overseas.

The national headquarters for the USO stayed in New York, with regional and state directors working closely together. In Nebraska, K.B. Cary was the chairman of Nebraska's USO committee, and Frank Finley was the regional director. There was a county chairman in each Nebraska county (ninety-three counties in all), as well as a treasurer and campaign and publicity chairs. Each community also had a local chairman. For example, in Morrill County, every community—Bridgeport, Broadwater, Angora and Redington—had a chairman. The Civilian Defense Committee Chair of each county usually appointed the county chair.

In 1942, a nationwide campaign to raise funds for the USO began with the goal of raising $32 million. Each Nebraska county was given a quota to meet based on population. For example, Morrill County had a smaller population than Scotts Bluff County and was given a quota of $400 (it raised $540.44), while Scotts Bluff County's quota was $3,300 (it raised exactly $3,300).[320]

Setting up USO centers was crucial to keeping up servicemen's morale. Sometimes temporary buildings were used until a bigger facility could be located. In Lincoln in June 1942, volunteers hurried to find a place to house the USO in anticipation of welcoming the nine thousand men set to be stationed at the Lincoln Air Base in late June and early July. Regional Director Frank Finley said, "We will need at least 20,000 square feet…and experience has shown that day rooms are best patronized if they are on the street floor. Central location is another important factor." Once they selected a building, it would take only about three weeks to get the center up and running. In addition, Lincoln also needed to provide a separate USO center for the black soldiers who would also be stationed at the Lincoln Air Base.[321] The Lincoln USO temporarily set up headquarters using the chamber of commerce rooms, but by October 19, 1942, the new space was undergoing remodeling and was open for business. Once completed, the center included a lounge, a writing center, two music rooms, game rooms, a kitchen, a pantry, service rooms, small parlors, a snack bar, a dance floor, showers and wash rooms and a powder room for the ladies.[322] The USO for the black soldiers opened a temporary, one-room location at 204 South Twelfth Street and moved into a new location in October 1943 at 212 South Twelfth Street.

Soldiers stationed at the Lincoln Air Base wrote letters gushing about the USO center and the city of Lincoln itself. One soldier wrote to his parents, "If anyone ever asks you about Lincoln, Neb....tell them it really is a swell place. If I could always be stationed in a place like this, I'd be the happiest guy in the world. Everyone treats us like we were kings, and does everything possible to make it enjoyable for us soldiers."[323] More than eight hundred volunteers helped the USO in Lincoln, both men and women, and made it their mission to give soldiers a "home away from home." In this they were incredibly successful.

At the Scottsbluff service club, the men stationed at the Scottsbluff air base were equally enthusiastic in their comments. "It's a swell place!" one said, while another commented, "A guy can have one grand time there." A committee made up solely of women ran the service center. About twelve to fourteen junior hostesses were on duty every day to dance with the men and play cards or ping pong.[324] At the Hebron USO, the committee in charge of the USO was made up of a group of women called the "Wingettes." Since it was a smaller location housed in Hebron's Masonic building, weekly activities were held instead of nightly ones for the soldiers at the nearby Bruning Air Base.[325]

In Omaha, a USO service center was set up at Union Station. With thousands of troops traveling through the center, it saw a great deal of use, and once again, women stepped up to meet the demand. An article in the Omaha World-Herald in 1944 reported, "Activity at the Union Station Service Men's Center is the continual state of affairs with patriotic women answering its pleas for unselfish devotion."[326] Earlier, in December 1943, the center received a citation from the 7th Service Command "for meritorious wartime service."[327] Perhaps one of the more memorable moments occurred in May 1945 when a train pulled into Omaha with 280 men, women and children, all former prisoners held in the Philippines by the Japanese. Some of the former POWs made their way to the Service Center. "Canteen workers took one look at their gaunt faces and brought out loaves of homemade bread and a freshly-baked ham contributed by Clifton Hill School."[328] Like the North Platte Canteen, food donations came from Omaha and the surrounding communities to support the center. And like the North Platte Canteen, letters from servicemen who visited the center at Union Station wrote letters expressing their admiration and thanks for the wonderful treatment they received.

One of the most successful women's organizations within the USO in Nebraska was the Lincolnettes. Based in Lincoln, this group of female hostesses for the servicemen in Lincoln began in May 1942. Organized by Mrs. Clifford Jorgensen, the group grew from just under 1,000 girls to nearly 1,200 girls in 1944. It was sponsored by the Lincoln Municipal Defense Council, the Lincoln Community Chest and the Lincoln Recreation Board. Their goal, as outlined in their archival documents, was as follows:

> TheLincolnettesorganizationisdesignedtoassembletogetheragroupof Lincolngirlswhomeetagoodstandardof conduct,whowillbewilling toserveaspartnersandhostessesinrecreationalactivitiesforservicemen stationedinLincoln,andwhowillagreetoabidebytherulesassetupfor the organization.[329]

To recruit members, the group sent notices to employers and businesses, announcing that it was looking for young women to help boost the morale of servicemen. Girls had to be at least eighteen years old, citizens of the United States and high school graduates. They filled out an application form and were then interviewed by the committee. If they were selected, they also had to agree to follow the rules. The group functioned like a small army, with each girl called a "cadet" and "six divisions headed by a colonel, and ten companies headed by captains. The cadet's guest card contains her division and company number and she must present it to enter Lincolnette functions." All six colonels were married women who also participated in other war activities. After a cadet had "served" for six to eight weeks, and if she had followed the rules, she received a permanent certificate. They also wore a white wings emblem with an "L" in the middle.[330]

The Lincolnette rules were simple yet strict. Girls had to dress appropriately in "class A" attire, which meant that no slacks, coats, anklets or hats could be worn to parties. Instead, the girls were encouraged to wear dresses and skirts. While on duty, they could not smoke on the dance floor, drink or have their own date. They also could not leave the service club with a serviceman. Above all, "Lincolnettes are to assume the responsibility of a recreational hostess so that the service men will feel at home and enjoy their stay in our community." Those who violated the rules or who did not attend the required four out of eight activities could be "dropped" from the group but could be considered for "reinstatement."[331]

Despite the rather strict rules, some in the community did not view the Lincolnettes favorably. A letter to local columnist Mary Gordon from

A troop train arrives at the North Platte Canteen. Lincoln County Historical Museum, North Platte, Nebraska.

a young woman named Gerry asked how she could help the war effort. "The type of girls in the Lincolnettes are, as many have told me, not the ones I care to associate with." Gordon sought to correct the young woman's viewpoint. "You are misinformed about the Lincolnettes," she wrote, "They are a good cross-section of Lincoln womanhood. Most of them are business girls and many of them feel they are really doing their bit to help the war effort by contributing their time one or two nights a week to dancing with soldiers."[332] A few days later, another letter to Mary Gordon from "Two Lincolnettes" further set the record straight. They wrote, "[W]e decided to write and add our bit to the fact that Gerry has been very misinformed about the Lincolnettes." The two writers went on to say that the dances were "supervised" and that only the "finest girls" attended.[333]

Although it is impossible to discern the origins of the gossip surrounding the Lincolnettes, the social mores of the time increased many people's worries about single women and the thousands of soldiers who descended on Lincoln and, indeed, military bases around the country. Women serving in the armed forces, like the WAACs, faced similar discrimination.

In 1943, a smear campaign arose against the WAACs, questioning their morality, with rumors swirling that 90 percent of them were prostitutes or were deliberately spreading venereal disease. It greatly affected the morale of the organization. Historian Leisa D. Meyer wrote that these rumors were a direct reflection of long-held notions "that only immoral women would associate with the military, and that the only valuable service a woman could provide the military was sexual in nature."[334] Perhaps those degrading the Lincolnettes held this same type of attitude, or perhaps they were worried about the soldiers' influence on the girls themselves. Another advice column, "Minerva's Mail," received a letter from a girl named Evelyn who wanted to join the Lincolnettes. After responding to one mother who'd lamented the bad influence of the airmen, she thought it would be a good idea to give the soldiers a fair chance. She also said, "I think it is a grand thing the girls [Lincolnettes] are doing to entertain the soldiers, and I would like to help. If the boys had enough things to do with the proper chaperonage, the Lincoln mother would not have to worry about the bad influence of the soldier on her daughter."[335]

Two officers at the Lincoln Army Air Base were very impressed with the group. One remarked how, compared to other places where he'd been stationed, the Lincolnettes' hospitality was superior. "It seems to be original with your community," he said. The other officer said that the Lincolnettes were known outside of Nebraska and had the reputation of being a "fine group of girls."[336]

The Lincolnettes were incredibly successful. Not only did they help at the USO, but they also participated in other activities around town. They had a group that visited servicemen at the air base hospital, held dances and picnics in Antelope Park and also went out to the air base several times for dances and other events. The Lincoln newspapers regularly featured their activities, and they never lacked for volunteers in their ranks. The program officially ended in November 1945.

Overall, Nebraska women volunteers put their best foot forward during the war, welcoming soldiers and airmen into their communities, fundraising and using their special skill set to "do their part" for the war effort, whether it was baking, sewing, dancing or organizing. They made a lasting impact on thousands of military men and women.

Chapter 9

NOTABLE NEBRASKANS

T housands of Nebraskans served during World War II in a variety of ways—on the homefront, in the military, as war correspondents, as innovators, as nurses and so much more. Every single Nebraskan can be proud of his or her dedication to serving the country. Some, however, made national and even international news for their contributions to the war effort. Others made quiet contributions that remained unacknowledged until well after the war was over. Evelyn Sharp from Ord, Nebraska, became one of the original WASPs (Women Airforce Service Pilots) and tragically died while ferrying a P-38 Lightning plane in April 1944. John Falter, who grew up in Falls City, Nebraska, was a magazine illustrator who drew covers for the Saturday Evening Post and during his service in the U.S. Navy designed some of the most famous propaganda posters for the homefront.

Two Nebraskans in particular made significant contributions and thus are profiled here. Ben Kuroki, a Japanese American man from Hershey, Nebraska, fought racism and prejudice simply to be allowed to serve his nation in the armed forces. Andrew Higgins, a hot-headed inventor from Columbus, Nebraska, designed the Higgins boat, which made possible the D-Day landings at Normandy in June 1944.

BEN KUROKI: FIGHTING A WAR ON TWO FRONTS

After serving fifty-eight combat missions for the U.S. Army Air Corps in the European and Pacific theaters of war, Ben Kuroki came home determined to wage his fifty-ninth—and most important—mission: fighting racism and bigotry. Kuroki knew the logistics well, having lived through far too many incidents of racism after the attack on Pearl Harbor. Only one of those incidents happened in Nebraska (a local farmer eyed him skeptically and said something derogatory about the Japanese), but the wartime fear against Japanese Americans and Japanese immigrants had swept from its origins on the West Coast across the rest of the nation. Ben resolved to use his voice and experiences to speak out against it. Some, though, didn't like his message.

Japanese American citizen Ben Kuroki fought fifty-eight combat missions for the U.S. Army Air Corps in the European and Pacific theaters of war. San Diego Air and Space Museum; no known copyright restrictions.

Born on a potato farm near Gothenburg on May 16, 1917, as one of ten children, Ben moved with his family to a farm near Hershey, Nebraska, when he was only a year old. His Japanese-born parents, Shosuke and Naka (née Yokoyama) Kuroki, struggled to raise their family, and Ben grew up poor. But in that small Nebraska town, he did not know prejudice. He grew up with friends of different ethnicities—Swedes, Italians, Mexicans, Germans and more—and he served as vice-president of his senior class, graduating in 1936. For a few years, he drove a truck across the country, delivering vegetables, hoping to make his fortune. But the attack on Pearl Harbor changed everything.

That very next day, Ben and his brother Fred, encouraged by their father, went to the recruiting station at North Platte and enlisted. They waited for a letter giving them their orders, but it never came. The recruiting sergeant told them there was a new regulation prohibiting Japanese from enlisting, but that didn't stop the brothers. Instead, they drove 150 miles to Grand Island specifically to enlist in the U.S. Army Air Corps.[337]

The brothers were sent to basic training at Fort Leavenworth and Sheppard Field near Wichita Falls, Texas, and immediately encountered racism. Other recruits casually used the term "Jap," while some thought they were Chinese and called them "Chinks." Ben and Fred were treated as pariahs. "It seemed like everybody was cold," Ben remembered later. "Maybe I was self-conscious but it kind of got to working on my mind."[338] Ben cried himself to sleep more than once. Kuroki said that he and Fred were "the loneliest boys in the U.S. Army" and that he would "rather go through all those bombing missions again" before reliving those training days.[339]

After their orders came through, the brothers were separated—Fred to the engineering corps and Ben to the air corps clerical school at Fort Logan, Colorado, for four months. Here he was able to make a few friends before he moved on to the 409th Squadron of the 93rd Bombardment Group at Barksdale Field, Louisiana. But once in Louisiana, he was put on twenty-one straight days of KP duty, peeling potatoes. He didn't dare go near the beautiful B-24 planes on the runway, terrified that he might be mistakenly shot as a saboteur.[340]

When it came time for his unit to go overseas, Ben's name wasn't on the list. He panicked. Fred had been kicked out of the air corps and sent to the army, where he was stuck digging ditches. Ben was terrified of the same happening to him. He certainly hadn't joined the military to be stuck in the United States as a typing clerk. Uncaring that he had tears in his eyes, Ben begged to be able to go with his unit, and as luck would have it, the officers in charge approved his request. He'd done it, and soon enough he was a on a ship to England. But his fight to be in combat wasn't over.

Though part of the first B-24 bomber group in England, Ben wasn't allowed to fly but was instead relegated to a desk job. Of course, such details didn't deter him. He volunteered for gunnery training in his spare time, and after much persistence, he was finally assigned to a crew that had lost one of its gunners. The pilot, Jake Epting, had previously asked his crew if they'd mind having a Japanese man serve with them. None objected, and Ben finally had a shot at fighting the Axis in the air.[341] Ben was promoted to a buck sergeant on December 6, 1942.[342]

For Ben's first mission, the crew of the Red Ass (the nose art featured a red donkey kicking Hitler in the chin) was sent to temporary duty in North Africa, close to Oran. Before the mission, Ben wrote a letter to his parents: "I just wanted to write and tell you how happy I am right now. Everybody is treating me just wonderful and tomorrow I'm finally getting a chance to prove myself."[343] During that first mission, Ben more than proved himself: he saved the life of one of his crew members. An explosion rocked the plane, and the tail gunner, Sergeant Elmer Dawley, was hit in the head by shrapnel and knocked unconscious. Another crew member was about to administer a shot of morphine, but Ben intervened. He'd learned in basic training that administering morphine to someone who was unconscious was deadly. Dawley would go on to recover, but he was out of the war for the time being—Ben took his place as tail gunner.[344]

A transfer to a base in Libya plus several more missions followed. Ben soon earned the nickname "Most Honorable Son," and it stuck. But on the way back to England, their plane ran out of gas and they crash-landed in Spanish Morocco. Since Spain was neutral, they were to be interned for the duration of the war in Melilla with the Spanish Air Corps. Worried that his ethnicity might spell trouble, Ben escaped and walked for two days, even going so far as to wrap a white T-shirt around his head as a turban in an attempt to blend in with the locals. But he was soon captured and sent back to prison with the rest of his crew. Fortunately, the crew was moved to a mountain town northeast called Alhama de Aragon and kept in a hotel for three months as "internees" rather than prisoners of war.[345] However, hotel living and loafing during the day didn't appeal to Kuroki and the rest of the crew, and they itched to get back into the fight.

The U.S. government pulled some strings and supposedly agreed to pay a brand-new Buick car to the Spanish government for their release. After a short stop in Gibraltar, Ben and three of his crew members were back in England.[346] Although Kuroki's career had made the news in Nebraska and nationally, his imprisonment in Spain didn't make any headlines, undoubtedly due to wartime censorship. In a 2015 interview with the National World War II Museum, Kuroki said that his imprisonment was "no big deal." But he also said that his time being interned probably saved his life. When he returned to England in 1943, he hardly recognized anyone in his outfit, as casualties had been so heavy during this part of the war.[347]

Kuroki and his crew jumped right back into bombing missions but soon began training for a particularly significant one: the bombing of the Ploesti oil refineries in Romania. These refineries were strategically important because they "produced most of the gasoline, diesel fuel, and other oil products used by Axis forces in the Mediterranean."[348] It was Ben's twenty-fourth mission and an incredibly dangerous one at that, with the bombers flying at treetop level. Kuroki said it was "absolutely terrifying." During one point in the raid, a huge storage tank exploded directly in his plane's path, and the flames shot higher than the plane, which was flying at only two hundred feet. "I could feel the heat penetrating my top turret dome," Kuroki said. "It was almost unbearable. It's a miracle we didn't catch on fire…it was unbelievable." When Kuroki and his crew got back to base, only two planes from the original nine in their squadron had returned. "I don't know why we made it, but we did," Kuroki said.[349]

The mission was costly. Aviation historian Walter J. Boyne later wrote, "Fully 30 percent of the airmen didn't make it home that day: Of the original 1,765 airmen who went airborne for the raid, 532 were either dead, prisoners, missing, or interned."[350]

At that time, bomber crews only had to complete twenty-five missions before they were eligible to go home. Kuroki flew his twenty-fifth mission and then did something extraordinary: he volunteered for five more. "Those five are for my kid brother," Kuroki said in an interview with Walter Cronkite. "I'm going to get at least one Jerry for him."[351] But Kuroki was compelled to extend his stay for more than shooting down a German plane for his brother. He wanted to do it for his fellow Nisei, those who hadn't been as fortunate as he had and were interned in camps. He wanted to prove how much he despised fascism. But most of all, he wanted to fight back against the racism and bigotry that had plagued his entire army career.

Kuroki's superiors approved his request. Since Ben's old crew had served its twenty-five missions and was on its way home, Kuroki had to find a new crew. He served with the crew of Lieutenant Homer Moran, aka "Chief," a full-blooded Sioux Native American from South Dakota.[352] On his last mission, Kuroki had a close call. While over Munster, Germany, the radio operator pulled on Kuroki's pant leg, and Ben leaned down to see what he wanted. At that moment, flak hit Kuroki's turret bubble, puncturing a hole in the glass-like dome. The force of it rendered Kuroki unconscious, and the radio man pulled him into the plane's belly. When Kuroki woke, he didn't have a scratch on him. If the radio man had not tugged his pant leg, Kuroki would have been killed.[353]

With Kuroki having completed thirty missions, the U.S. Army Air Corps sent him home on furlough, and to his astonishment, he was treated like a hero. Newspaper stories, radio interviews and speaking engagements filled his schedule. Of course, not everyone was thrilled. In California, Ben was scheduled to be on a radio program with Hollywood actress and singer Ginny Sims. Unfortunately, they canceled his appearance. The producer apologized, saying, "Somebody in the NBC executive department has the bright idea that the Japanese American question is too controversial. They won't let you on the air."[354] Deflated and angry, he wanted to cancel his upcoming speech in front of six hundred people at the posh Commonwealth Club in San Francisco but was refused. Incredibly nervous, he got up to speak, faltering at first but then growing in confidence as he talked about his service, about democracy and patriotism and about being an American. When he finished talking, he was astonished to see everyone stand up and applaud. In fact, his audience was so impressed with his talk that he had to return to the stage twice. Magazines and newspapers printed his speech, and he began receiving letters from around the country.[355]

But the small digs made him think that he hadn't done enough to prove his loyalty. He itched to go to the Pacific and take the fight to Japan. But the American press continued to cover his story and notably used "Jap" when describing him, especially in the headlines. Indeed, the famous war correspondent (and later news anchor) Walter Cronkite wrote an article about Kuroki in November 1943 and used several unflattering stereotypes to describe him: "Ben Kuroki has slant eyes. His skin is sallow, yellow. He is tiny. Ben Kuroki certainly looks Japanese."[356] No matter that Cronkite turned the narrative around by praising Kuroki's fighting spirit and feats of heroism; the fact remains that Cronkite, as so many others during that period, used racist language.

Anti-Japanese sentiment had existed in America for decades, stretching back to the 1890s and continuing the anti-Chinese prejudice that had started in early California in the 1840s. One key feature of this prejudice was known as the "yellow peril." As Jacobus tenBroek, Edward N. Barnhart and Floyd W. Matson wrote in their study on the Japanese American internment, Prejudice, War, and the Constitution, "From the beginning it was alleged that the Chinese had only hatred for American institutions, that their sole loyalty was to the homeland and the emperor. Their entrance into the states was seen as an 'invasion' and their motive ultimate conquest of the country by of [sic] Asia, eyeing the North American continent."[357] As Japanese immigrants began arriving in America, many people confused the two nationalities. Soon, the Japanese were seen as worse than the Chinese. "From the beginning the Japanese was tagged, like his predecessor, as 'tricky, unreliable, and dishonest.' In flagrant contradiction of all evidence, he was accused of fomenting crime, menacing white women, and generally scoffing at Western concepts of law and morality."[358]

This type of thinking was largely present on the Pacific coast, where most Japanese immigrants settled. Since Ben's father had moved to Nebraska, the Kuroki family did not encounter this type of prejudice simply because Nebraskans were not steeped in it. This is not to say, however, that this prejudice was confined to the West Coast. The anti-Japanese sentiment was endemic to all of the United States, but it was most keenly felt and expressed on the West Coast.

In the 1930s, as word began to spread of Japan's aggression and war in the Pacific, prejudice continued to rumble under the surface. However, after Pearl Harbor, "the traditional charges were widely revived and the stereotype recalled in detail; public attitudes toward the Japanese minority soon crystallized around the well-worn themes of treachery and disloyalty, and expressions of opinion came more and more to be characterized by suspicion, fear, and anger."[359]

This, then, was what Kuroki faced. But even after all of his accomplishments—being awarded the Distinguished Flying Cross among other citations, successfully completing thirty missions and finding acceptance and friendship with his crew members—it still wasn't enough to convince many Americans that their prejudice against Japanese Americans was flat out wrong.

And nowhere was that prejudice more on display than in the Japanese American "relocation" camps. Worried that Japanese Americans constituted a threat, President Roosevelt issued Executive Order 9066 on February 19, 1942. All persons of Japanese ancestry from the West Coast states were forced to evacuate and move to hastily built camps. These camps were miserable, often placed in barren landscapes and were a clear violation of Japanese Americans' civil rights. These people lost businesses, homes and possessions.

After Kuroki's stint of speechmaking ended, the U.S. War Department ordered him to visit three Japanese American internment camps to help bolster enlistment to the 442nd Infantry Regiment. Composed entirely of Japanese American soldiers, this regiment was created in March 1943 and began fighting in Italy in June 1944.

Dissident internees resisted the call to join the 442nd, upset that the government wanted them to fight at the same time they were refusing them their civil rights. The War Department hoped that Kuroki's example would ease this negative attitude, and he visited Heart Mountain War Relocation Center in Cody, Wyoming; Minidoka War Relocation Camp in Idaho; and the Topaz War Relocation Center in Utah. While many of the younger generation saw him as something of a Hollywood star, wanting his autograph and posing for pictures with him, the older generation felt just the opposite. "The older generation didn't have any respect for me," Kuroki said. Nevertheless, he spoke to the dissident group, accompanied by extra guards. "Outside of a couple hissing and booing's, there wasn't any violence," Kuroki said, but "their leader called me names." Kuroki later said he "didn't enjoy the experience."[360]

Not only did he not enjoy making speeches and being the center of attention, but Kuroki also had difficulty seeing his fellow Japanese Americans behind barbed wire. Fortunately, his family didn't have to endure internment because they were from Nebraska. But Kuroki undoubtedly wondered how he would have felt about fighting for the U.S. government if he, too, had been interned and had everything taken away from him. It was a sobering thought.[361]

Even though Kuroki had been feted by Hollywood stars and welcomed by powerful California businessmen, the prejudice continued. When in Denver to visit his sister, he went to grab a taxi cab, and the man inside said, "I won't ride with no lousy Jap."[362] The experience soured him, and later he said he never wanted to go to Denver again.

Then terrible news came. His best friend from Hershey, Gordy Jorgenson, had been killed fighting in the Solomon Islands in the Pacific. That, as well as his stubborn determination to prove his loyalty, only made him more resolute than ever to fight in the Pacific. He even decided to join the Omaha branch of the Veterans of Foreign Wars in November 1944, becoming the first Nisei member.

Kuroki was sent back to training to a B-29 base in Harvard, Nebraska. He found a new crew piloted by James Jenkins, and none of them had a problem flying with a Japanese American. He waited for word giving him the clearance to take the fight directly to Japan, only to once again have his hopes dashed. The U.S. War Department refused, pointing to its policy prohibiting Japanese Americans from flying in B-29s. In a 2015 interview, Kuroki said, "I had to fight like hell for the right to fight for my country, and the biggest fight of all was taking on the War Department."[363]

With the War Department still denying him his chance to fight in the Pacific, Kuroki's friends began bombarding the department with letters and telegrams. Dr. Monroe Deutsch, vice-president of the University of California, personally sent a telegram to Secretary of War Henry Stimson, as did the president of Stanford University and the editor of the San Francisco Chronicle. Mrs. Ruth Kingman of the Committee on American Principles and Fair Play sent a telegram that read, "This committee feels that the future of our loyal Americans of Japanese ancestry depends considerably upon the Army's unqualified recognition of courageous services of Kuroki and other Nisei war heroes. We respectfully urge that Kuroki be assigned to his duties on the same basis as the other members of the air corps."[364]

Major Erickson at the Colorado Air Base also wrote a glowing recommendation letter, saying, "His background, attainments, courage and zeal to participate in the war against the Japanese Empire leaves no doubt of his patriotism and fidelity to his native land, the United States of America."[365] Kuroki even personally visited U.S. Representative Carl Curtis at his home in Minden, Nebraska, and asked him to intercede on his behalf. In 1991, Curtis recalled, "I decided to appeal to the chief of staff, General George Marshall, and I dispatched a telegram to him."[366]

It worked. On November 16, 1944, Ben received a letter from Secretary of War Henry Stimson via Dr. Deutsch, granting him permission to fight in the Pacific. Ecstatic, his crew named the plane Honorable Sad Saki and prepared to fly overseas as part of the 505th bomb group. They were nearly derailed when an FBI agent and a military intelligence officer, who obviously hadn't been privy to Secretary Stimson's decision, tried to take Kuroki off the plane right before takeoff. Fortunately, Kuroki kept the letter from Stimson in his bag and was able to show the officials that, yes, he had a right to be there.[367] Once again, Ben had faced a battle with prejudice and won.

From his base on Tinian in the Mariana Islands, Kuroki had to take extra precautions. In an early 1945 letter to C.F. Mulvihill, tenth district VFW judge advocate in Omaha, Kuroki wrote, "There are still a few of my dishonorable ancestors running loose on this island. They don't give us much trouble, but at one time our boys fell victims to a lot of wild rumors and became a bit trigger happy....I had to be careful not to go walking in my sleep or some yardbird would take a couple of shots at me." He then continued, "I must concentrate on dropping some 'roses' on Tokyo Rose. If things go well, I'll see you in Omaha again."[368]

The pressure of flying so many missions, of facing prejudice at home, of fighting for his right to fight and of worrying about the possibility of what would happen to him if the Japanese took him prisoner started taking its toll. Nightmares plagued Kuroki, and it was getting harder to sleep. After flying ten missions against Japan, Kuroki and his crew were sent to Honolulu for rest and relaxation. It did the trick, and soon Kuroki was back on bombing missions, dropping incendiaries at night on Tokyo, Yokohama, Osaka and more. Curiously, there was a plane sitting at their base named the Enola Gay, but it wasn't until later that he found out why. Finally, after flying twenty-eight missions in the Pacific, Kuroki was done.

Ironically, the night he returned from his last mission, he was almost killed by a drunken fellow serviceman who called him a "damned Jap." After so many times of turning the other cheek and enduring racial slurs, Kuroki couldn't let this insult stand. He exploded. Next thing he knew, the drunken serviceman slashed him across the top of the head with a bayonet. Bleeding profusely, Kuroki was taken to the hospital, where he received twenty-four stitches. While in the hospital, the truth of the Enola Gay's presence on their base became clear when the atomic bomb was dropped on Hiroshima. The war was over.

Since he was still in the hospital, Kuroki was not able to fly home with his crew. Instead, he had to wait for a liberty ship to make the slow journey back to America. It took twenty-one days for the ship to reach San Francisco. "When I saw the Golden Gate Bridge, that was the most beautiful sight in the world, and I realized I'd survived the war," Kuroki later recalled. But as soon as he arrived in San Francisco, the War Department whisked him away to New York and delivered him to the Waldorf Astoria Hotel to appear on the New York Herald Tribune Forum with General George C. Marshall. He hadn't changed his uniform in twenty-one days and asked to be delivered to the hotel's back door.

Perhaps the most memorable moment of the forum, however, came when General Jonathan Wainwright, the highest-ranking American POW held by Japan, shook his hand. Ben, it seemed, had come full circle.[369]

It would be a while before Kuroki could leave the military and resume his civilian life. The War Department continued to use him for publicity purposes, and he went on another tour throughout the United States, giving speeches and radio shows. A correspondent for Yank magazine, Ralph Martin, wrote a biography of him (released in 1946), and he received letters from all across the United States. Kuroki realized that the country still had a long way to go in terms of accepting people of different races. Thus, he made a decision.

In November 1945, he appeared on the radio program American Town Meeting of the Air and said, "I've had fifty-eight combat missions and I'm pretty tired. My hands still shake a little but I've got one more mission to go. There is still the fight against prejudice and race hatred. I call it my fifty-ninth mission, and I have a hunch that's one mission I won't be fighting alone."[370]

Once out of the military, Kuroki started this mission, financed entirely on his own, and he continued to travel around the country, delivering speeches and drawing awareness to his cause. While in Utah, he met a woman named Shige and fell in love. They married, and once the funds for his tour ran out, they moved to Lincoln, where Ben used the GI Bill to attend the University of Nebraska in 1947. He studied journalism, believing that it would "equip him to carry on his struggle in a different and perhaps more effective way."[371] After graduation, Kuroki bought a newspaper in York, Nebraska, the first

Japanese American in Nebraska to do so. In the ensuing years, Kuroki worked on several other newspapers, eventually moving to California, where he continued to be a newspaper man. He and his wife remained there for the rest of their lives. But his exploits in World War II were never forgotten. He had received three Distinguished Flying Crosses and an Air Medal with five oak leaf clusters. In 2005, he was awarded the Distinguished Service Medal. He visited President George W. Bush three times, and one included a special Asian American meeting at the White House, where Kuroki and the president saluted each other.[372]

The honors continued to roll in. He received the Nebraska Press Association's highest honor, the President's Award, and the University of Nebraska awarded him a Doctor of Letters, its highest honorary degree. In addition, the university created the Ben Kuroki Journalism Scholarship. Kuroki also received the Audie Murphy Award in 2010. But Kuroki didn't just collect awards. Instead, he continued to volunteer his time to others, joining in the movement to ask Congress to award the Medal of Honor to the Nisei 442nd Regiment.

In 2007, Bill Kubota, whose father had been interned in a camp during the war, created a documentary on Kuroki called *Most Honorable Son*. It aired on Nebraska's PBS station, NETV, several times over the ensuing years.[373]

Kuroki passed away in 2015. His strength and determination to fight back against the prejudice of his time, to keep going despite the odds and to work hard and stay humble are all indicative of the Nebraska spirit. His legacy continues on, inspiring future generations to stay true to their core beliefs and, as Winston Churchill said, to "Never, never, never give up."

ANDREW JACKSON HIGGINS: D-DAY'S UNLIKELY HERO

Hot-headed, tough, inventive and skilled, Andrew Jackson Higgins emerged in the 1940s as head of one of the nation's largest industrial complexes. But for those who knew him growing up in Columbus and Omaha, Nebraska, it was no surprise. Even as a youth, Higgins showed extraordinary determination and shrewd business sense in whatever endeavor on which he embarked. He loved building boats and built one in the basement of his mother's home in Omaha at the age of twelve. However, when he finished, he discovered that it was too big to get out. So, he gathered some friends, removed part of the basement wall, retrieved the boat and then rebuilt the wall before his mother

Nebraska-born Andrew Higgins created a shipbuilding empire in New Orleans, Louisiana, and his Higgins boats made the D-Day invasion at Normandy successful. Wikimedia Commons.

returned home.[374] Such ingenuity and outright nerve would serve him well in the years to come.

Born in Columbus, Nebraska, on August 28, 1886, to John Gonegle and Annie Long O'Conor Higgins, Andrew was the youngest of ten children. His father died when he was only seven, and his mother moved the family to Omaha. Higgins showed little interest in school, often getting in trouble, but in 1900 he did enroll in Creighton High Prep School in Omaha, where he played football. He didn't finish, however, leaving after his junior year to join the 2nd Nebraska Infantry of the National Guard, commanded by William Jennings Bryan. After undergoing militia maneuvers in Nebraska and building a pontoon bridge, Higgins became fascinated by amphibious training and became a student of military history. He also spent two summers working in Wyoming logging camps. It was those two interests— boats and lumber—that led him to move to the South in 1906 when he was only twenty years old.[375]

Higgins settled near Mobile, Alabama, bought a farm and married Angele Leona Colsson in 1908. He started his own lumber business only to lose it to a hurricane, but his determination served him well. Thirsty for knowledge on business, timber and shipbuilding, he took several jobs over the next few years in those industries. In 1910, his family, which now included a young son, moved to New Orleans, where Higgins would stay the rest of his life.

Higgins started another business in 1916 called A.J. Higgins Lumber and Export Company and built schooners and brigantines to carry his lumber.[376] In 1930, he incorporated the business into Higgins Industries, but the Depression caused problems; he made several smart business decisions to keep him solvent. By 1937, his business was growing, and he had fifty employees, including highly qualified craftsmen.[377]

By this time, Higgins had four sons and two daughters. He deeply loved his family, and his daughter fondly remembered Sundays when the entire group—children and grandchildren—would gather together for dinner. The three oldest sons were instrumental in helping Higgins. The oldest, Ed, was the "mechanical genius of the family and served as the company's chief mechanic," while Andrew Jr. and Frank served as office manager and field superintendent, respectively.[378] Higgins concentrated on building "dependable, sturdy workboats," and since his market was far different than that on the eastern seaboard, he worked on creating rugged, shallow-bottomed craft. Through trial and error, Higgins eventually came up with the Eureka, a "spoonbill-bow" boat that became the "ancestor" to the Higgins boats used during the war.

A nine-page story in Life magazine described the Eureka as follows:

> [H]eincorporatedareversecurveonthebottomaftofamidships.The midshipssectionitselfhebuiltintheshapeofaV.Thiscombinationshot outtheaeratedwaterfromthesidesoftheboatandleftsolidwaterinthe semitunnel.Notonlywasspeedpracticallydoubled,butthesolidwateracted asakindofrail,enablingtheboattobeturnedsafelyalmostinitsown length.SoHigginsnowhadashallow-waterboatasfastandconsiderably moremaneuverablethananordinaryboat.Itcouldalsojumpspits,sandbars andlogs,couldrushuponabeachand,withonlypartofthepropellerin water, back off and turn around before the next big wave broke.[379]

To eliminate the problem of leaks after sitting in the hot tropical sun for months, Higgins had "constructed a double-bottom boat with a piece of canvas between the layers. The idea of using canvas to prevent leakage was not new, but the concept of interlocking the corners of the chine and the keel was developed by Higgins Industries."[380] The Eureka became immensely popular during the late 1930s, with numerous oil companies and South American governments purchasing them for use, as well as the U.S. Army Corps of Engineers and the Coast Guard. By 1941, having tested and honed his designs, plus improved the Eureka, Higgins Industries had two plants and 1,600 employees and was making PT (patrol torpedo) boats and landings crafts for the British in their fight against Hitler. Higgins was also making PT boats, LCPLs (landing craft personnel large), LCVPs (landing craft vehicle personnel), LCP (landing craft personnel) and LCMs (landing craft mechanized) for the U.S. Navy.[381] He also established the Higgins Boat Operators and Marine Engine Maintenance School to train the U.S. Navy, Coast Guard and Marine Corps. He also fully funded it. Thus, Higgins was already working with the U.S. military when Pearl Harbor was bombed and soon had contracts with the U.S. Army and the U.S. Army Air Corps.

"The sad state of war," Higgins said, "has made it my duty to build." His production increased tremendously, as did his business, going from two plants to eight and more than twenty thousand workers. With this labor force, he was able to produce seven hundred boats per month. But not only was Higgins innovative in terms of design, he also treated his employees fairly no matter the color of his or her skin. "Higgins became an equal-opportunity employer by default," wrote Douglas Brinkley, "hiring women, blacks, the elderly, the handicapped—anyone he could find to build boats. Everyone who had the same job was paid the same wage." In fact, Higgins Industries regularly won the Army-Navy "E," the U.S. government's highest award for a company.[382]

The year 1943 was a banner time for Higgins. Not only had he been awarded an honorary degree at Creighton University, but he'd also built the Higgins-Tucker Engine Factory and standardized the LCVP so it officially became known as the Higgins boat. Even Adolf Hitler knew who Andrew Higgins was, calling him the "new Noah." The boats produced by Higgins Industries had been instrumental in amphibious landings such as the U.S. 5th Army's landings at Salerno, Italy, and in helping with General Douglas MacArthur's forces in capturing Salamaua in New Guinea and the invasion of Guadalcanal in 1942. In fact, according to Douglas Brinkley, by September 1943, 92 percent of U.S. naval vessels were built by Higgins Industries.[383] It was an astonishing feat.

Why were these boats so effective? The National World War II Museum in New Orleans summarizes it well:

Higgins Boats changed the way that war was fought. Previously, navies would have to attack ports, which were usually heavily defended. By using Higgins Boats, armies could unload across an open beach and have more options in choosing their attack points. This also stretched the defending

armies.Insteadof concentratingononlyafewentrypoints,defendershadto
covermoreshoreline.InboththePacificandEuropeanTheatersofWorld
War II, Higgins Boats allowed Allied armies to move ashore.[384]

The clearest demonstration of the usefulness and importance of the
Higgins boat came on June 6, 1944, the D-Day invasion at Normandy,
France. The Allied armada of more than 5,000 ships included 1,500 boats
made by Higgins Industries. Although the losses on the beaches were horrific,
the Higgins boat made it possible to land the Allied forces and, eventually, to
win the war. Later, Dwight Eisenhower, supreme commander of the Allied
Expeditionary Force in Europe, would tell historian Stephen Ambrose in
1964, "[Andrew Higgins] is the man who won the war for us. If Higgins had
not designed and built those landing craft, we never would have landed over
an open beach. The whole strategy of the war would have been different."[385]
High praise, indeed.

In addition to inventing, building and running a company, Higgins was
involved with politics at the highest level. He actively campaigned for
Franklin D. Roosevelt's election in 1944 and had pushed for Harry S Truman
to be on the ticket as Roosevelt's vice president. "[Higgins] saw Truman as
the one person in Washington who understood the needs of business and
who the nation could trust," Strahan wrote.[386] Higgins was also aware of
how fragile Roosevelt's health was and knew that Truman would make a
worthy successor. When Roosevelt easily won reelection, Higgins wrote to
Truman, "Thank God the country had good sense....I know you are glad
the campaign was over. It certainly was a stinker. This is the first time I ever
got active in political campaigning."[387]

Higgins's company had flourished in 1944 as well. He was producing his
boats and ships but also "wing panels, plywood, plastics, engines, solar stills,
pumps, torpedo tubes, radios, and a variety of other products." Higgins was
one of the biggest employers in Louisiana, paying more than $60 million in
wages annually. But he also had other projects unrelated to manufacturing. He
helped create housing for his workers and instituted a recreation program for
them as well. He appointed his sister Joy Montgomery Higgins to direct it, and
she was instrumental in having playgrounds built, constructing a child care
center and developing youth sports activities and classes in drama and music.
Higgins took pride in taking care of his workers' needs beyond the factories,
something many other major American companies could not claim.[388] Indeed,
one of Higgins's directors, Ted Sprague, remembered how much Higgins
wanted his employees involved with the company. Higgins encouraged his

foremen, superintendents and anyone else interested to stop by his office every afternoon after the first shift to discuss ideas and problems:

> We'djustsitinthereandtalk. Thatwayhereallyknewwhatwasgoing on.Helistened.Hemightraisehellafteryougotthroughtellinghimwhat youthought,buthelistened.Hehadabigego,buthedidn'tfeellikehe wassodamnsmarthecouldn'tlearnsomething.Ifyouknewsomethinghe didn'tknow,andyoutoldhim,thenhewashappytoknowit.Hedidn't put anybody down unless they got way out of line.[389]

After the war ended in Europe in May and later in the Pacific in August, Andrew Higgins had no plans to close up shop. A few of his plants shut their doors since there was no longer a need for such vast war production, but Higgins was nowhere near done designing and inventing. Unfortunately, he'd been embroiled in a labor dispute with the War Labor Board, the National Labor Relations board and unions. It became a story covered in newspapers across the nation. The dispute and labor strikes became so intense that Higgins closed some of his plants and began to liquidate Higgins Industries. With the war over, government contracts were canceled. It was the beginning of the end.

In early 1946, he created a new corporation that would "produce commercial boats, pleasure craft, and amphibious pop-up camp trailers."[390] In 1948, he got into the housing market with his Higgins Thermo-Con houses. But the damage had been done from the labor disputes and the end of the war. "The company's credit was so bad by now that it was on a C.O.D. basis with every supplier," Strahan wrote. "A company that had once employed over twenty thousand workers and had hundreds of millions of dollars' worth of contracts was by Christmas, 1948, down to seventy-five workers and unable to raise enough money to finish a single boat."[391]

Still, Higgins refused to quit. He managed to scrounge up a few contracts to keep the company going, and once he fulfilled those contracts, he managed to pay off his debts and have a reserve of $100,000. Then, salvation: the United States entered the Korean War conflict, and in November 1950, the U.S. Army Corps of Engineers awarded Higgins a $2 million contract to build lightweight aluminum boats. More government contracts came his way. Production increased, as did the number of employees. Higgins was surging back.

Unfortunately, Higgins didn't live long enough to see the completion of those government contracts. A diabetic who suffered from stomach ulcers, the sixty-five-year-old Higgins entered a hospital in New Orleans for a checkup, but problems arose. He died on August 1, 1952, from a stomach ailment, although one contemporary account said he suffered a fatal stroke.

Higgins's company, taken over by one of his sons, continued to operate for a number of years but never again rose to the same prominence it had during the war. The company no longer exists today.

Andrew Higgins's contribution to World War II was largely ignored for years until famed historian Stephen Ambrose worked to found a museum dedicated to D-Day on the very location in New Orleans where Higgins had tested his boats. Because Higgins Industries had been located in New Orleans, it was the perfect spot for a D-Day Museum. Today, the National World War II Museum is a world-class museum, offering educational programing, yearly symposia, oral histories and more on the American experience during World War II.

Nebraska has not forgotten Higgins. In his birthplace of Columbus, a memorial stands to the industrial giant, complete with a steel replica of a Higgins boat and a squad of bronze soldiers hitting the beach. Sand collected from numerous invasion beaches of World War II makes up that beach, a true testament to the vital role Higgins played in winning the war.[392]

Chapter 10

FEEDING THE NATION

Nebraska Agriculture

N o history of Nebraska during World War II would be complete without a discussion on agriculture. Since it is such a vast topic, however, one that could easily have its own book, a brief discussion will have to suffice for this work.

Agriculture forms the basis of the Nebraska economy today just as it did during the war years. Before America's entry into the war, the farm economy was dealing with a surplus of agricultural commodities, low prices and too much manpower. During the Great Depression, the government had taken on a larger role in the farming industry. The Agricultural Adjustment Administration replaced the Farm Board in 1933 with a goal of getting prices that would enable farmers to have the purchasing power they did in 1910–14. But all of the adjustment and supplementary programs didn't fix the price problems, which remained low. In addition, horsepower had declined sharply when farmers were able to buy tractors. This meant that more acreage could be farmed, which added to the surplus of farm products. Labor-saving machinery also decreased jobs and led to a surplus of farm labor. Other advances in technology—including new strains of seeds, improved livestock production and hybrid seed corn—helped increase market supplies.

When German U-boats began targeting U.S. ships en route to England and Europe in earnest in 1940, farming exports fell below Depression-era levels. The United States responded by sending in naval destroyers to combat the U-boats and keep shipping channels open, and in March 1941, the Lend-

Lease Act went into effect. Soon, equipment, weapons and food exports such as eggs, dairy products, canned vegetables, dry beans and pork were en route to the ports of America's war-torn Allies. Surplus commodities were quickly bought by the U.S. government, and farm income increased substantially.

When America entered World War II in December 1941, however, everything changed. American farmers now had to feed not only its allies but also the U.S. military and the American people. The government immediately went to work. The U.S. Department of Agriculture (USDA) swelled as new administrations and boards were created to handle farming issues. The War Food Administration coordinated and developed policies and procedures for food distribution and production. Farm prices were set by Congress and the Office of Price Administration (OPA). The OPA also controlled food distribution at the retail level. The War Production Board regulated the manufacturing of new farm machinery, and the War Manpower Commission dealt with labor issues.

But red tape and inefficiency plagued the USDA, and coordinating a well-balanced response remained difficult. An article in the April 6, 1942 edition of TIME noted that "U.S. farmers had the food situation well in their plow-calloused hands. They were doing better than the Washington food bureaucrats. A half-dozen Government agencies were dabbling in the food problem, with well-confused results."

Still, the farming industry was pivotal to winning the war. Secretary of Agriculture Claude R. Wickard coined the patriotic slogan "Food will win the war and write the peace." Soon, posters, pamphlets and even educational films flooded the country and the farm community itself. One short film from the dairy industry described milk as white ammunition. Posters specifically aimed at farmers touted, "They Need Food. Plant More Beans. Help Feed Those Freed from Axis Rule" and "Get your farm in the fight! Use conservation methods for bigger yields now." Pamphlets even gave tips on how to cut labor and suggested, "Eliminate unnecessary motions and steps in every chore" and "Take time and patience to train inexperienced helpers. Start them with simple tasks first."

Before the war, the surplus of agriculture workers had been a problem. But the role soon reversed. Most young, able-bodied men volunteered for war or found better-paying jobs in war industries in the cities. The 1940 draft had only put a small dent in farm labor, but after Pearl Harbor, it played a key role, taking men up to forty-five years old.

According to Iowa agricultural professor Walter W. Wilcox, "Between January 1940 and January 1945, an estimated five million people left farms for urban residences and the military services." The severe labor shortage became a key difficulty, and it wasn't until November 1942 that the government finally gave agriculture special consideration in military deferment with the Tydings Amendment. Those farm laborers volunteering for military service first had to have a certificate from their local draft board that noted they were not essential farm workers.[393]

But there was still a stigma attached to farmers not enlisting. An editorial in the Alliance Times-Herald in December 1942 profiled one local farmer who refused to apply for a deferment "because people will talk. I've got to live here after the war is over and I'm not going to have people point to me as a 'dodger.'" The editorial went on to speak on behalf of him and other farm laborers who refused deferments: "And unless the people in the rural communities, where these farmers live and will continue to live, recognize farm work as being as patriotic as work in the war industries and training camps there will be a critical food shortage that can result only in defeat no matter how many bonds we buy, how much material we make and how many troops we train."[394]

Despite those farmers who took deferments, the labor shortage became critical. It was partially relieved by school children and women helping out in the fields, but it did not receive significant relief until German and Italian POWs were approved as a labor force.

In addition to labor shortages, farmers were further impeded by the lack of new farm equipment. Many farm machinery manufacturers were converted to war industries, and the Office of Price Administration set strict quotas for the manufacture of new farm machinery. Instead of high production of new tractors, factories were urged to make more repair and maintenance parts. The government encouraged farmers to use every available piece of farm equipment. One International Harvester Company ad in early 1942 wanted farmers to order the parts they needed immediately so they could put "new life in your old equipment and make it work as never before."

Ironically, due to their increased income, farmers now had the money to afford new tractors. But finding one to buy wasn't easy. A black market even sprang up in response to the need.

Despite the country's concentration on vital war industries, agricultural innovation did occur. Research engineers continued to develop new machines and fine-tune models of existing machines. Smaller, more efficient tractors were developed, and labor-saving techniques improved other farm implements.

In a savvy marketing move, the Massey-Harris company approached the War Production Board with its prototype of a self-propelled combine. It wanted to use it in a new Harvest Brigade of farmers willing to harvest two thousand acres of wheat. Not only would this new combine decrease manpower, but there was also less waste involved during harvest. The board agreed and gave the manufacturer enough steel to produce five hundred combines over its quota. The machines were built and distributed to custom cutters who worked mostly in the Great Plains. The brigade was a huge success, and it also spurred a new industry: custom combining.

Food dehydration processes and fresh freezing of fruits and vegetables also became important since much of the food needed to be sent across the country or shipped overseas. The U.S. Thermo Control Company (now called Thermo King) created the refrigerated trailer that made transporting fresh foods much easier. Combined, these processes increased the time between when the food was harvested and when it was consumed, resulting in a much lower percentage of food spoiling. Air and truck transportation of farm products also increased.

Hog and cattle production saw a sharp increase during the war. By January 1942 in Nebraska, "The number of cattle also expanded from 3 to 3.2 million head, the value of which 'materially increased' from $43.10 to $53.80 per head."[395] The dairy industry saw huge changes, with farmers now being able to handle milk in bulk with new and improved automatic milking machines. However, advances in feed technology and breeding made it possible to have individual cows produce more milk, thus decreasing the size of dairy cows overall after 1944.

Previously little-used crops, like soybeans, made a huge impact during the war years. Although the legume had been introduced in America in the early 1900s, it was mostly imported from Asian countries. By 1918, about 169,000 acres had been planted. But by 1942, there were 14,241,000 acres in soybeans. The USDA called it the "miracle bean." Soybeans doubled as livestock feed, but they were mostly used for oil in shortening and other edible products. Without the increase in soybean production, wartime rationing of food fats would have been much more severe.

To supplement food rationing and ease the farmers' burden, the government encouraged Americans to plant Victory Gardens. Gardening became the new American pastime. According to the USDA, more than 20 million Victory Gardens were planted during the war. Seed companies, businesses, the government and magazine articles produced pamphlets and articles on how to plant the best Victory Garden. An article in the March

"Get Your Farm in the Fight!" Office for Emergency Management, Office of War Information, Domestic Operations Branch, Bureau of Special Services. U.S. National Archives, Identifier 514376.

1944 Ladies' Home Journal gave its readers an entire fifteen-point plan for a garden, including what type of vegetables to plant and how to arrange them. More propaganda posters appeared, saying, "A garden will make your rations go further" and "Grow a garden—it's thrifty. It's patriotic." Canning saw a substantial increase, and the sale of pressure cookers skyrocketed. Booklets and cookbooks with advice and recipes on how to cook using ration points also flooded the market. They placed emphasis on healthy, nutritious meals, a must for keeping fit so everyone could contribute to the war effort. The gardens made a difference. By 1944, about 40 percent of America's vegetables were grown in such gardens.[396]

One of the most important sources of news on farming for Nebraskans was Nebraska Farmer. Founded in 1859 (and still published today), the magazine kept farmers abreast of prices, best practices, new technology, what was happening in Washington, D.C. (the monthly feature on D.C. was written by "Our Washington Correspondent"), and more. During the World War II years, Nebraska Farmer hammered home the "Food will win the war" message, even running a monthly feature called "The Farm Front" that "has as its purpose the discussion of farm problems and topics brought about by the present emergency." In fact, the front cover of the March 7, 1942 issue stated, "Soldiers in Overalls: Prepare to Produce Food to Win the War and Write the Peace."

As the war came to an end, Nebraska farmers found themselves in even more demand, as they were now producing food for a devastated European population. To avoid the kind of recession in the farming industry experienced after World War I, the government extended price controls on agricultural commodities for two years. Relief efforts—like the United Nations Relief and Rehabilitation Administration, the Marshall Plan and the Berlin Airlift—were critical to getting war-torn Europe and Japan back on their feet. Food exports stayed high, and farmers once again profited, leading to an economic boom. Compared to $3.5 billion in 1940, total net farm income in 1947 was $15.4 billion.

Overall, Nebraska farmers profited economically from the war, pulling them out of the Depression years. As R. Douglas Hurt wrote, "They paid off debts, retired mortgages, bought land, and saved."[397] The United States had asked farmers for help in winning the war, and Nebraska farmers rose to the occasion.

CONCLUSION

As part of the Great Plains, Nebraska often finds itself being referred to as "Flyover Country." The implication is that not much happens here and, thus, it can be dismissed as being of any importance. But this is a mistake. During World War II, Nebraska had an immense role to play in the fight against the Axis powers, and Nebraskans fulfilled their duty and more.

Perhaps it was due to Nebraskans' pioneer and immigrant spirit, the grit and determination needed to plow the unforgiving land and tame it into a prosperous, productive home. Nebraskans' work ethic was unrelenting, as it still is today, and during a time of war, it was exactly what the United States needed to win.

Nebraskans of all ages contributed to the war effort and put the Cornhusker State on the national stage. From welcoming troops and providing them a home away from home to toiling long hours at war plants and farm fields, planting Victory Gardens, gathering scrap and raising money for war bonds, Nebraskans did all they could to help win the war. As this work amply shows, Nebraskans can be proud of their wartime legacy, one that continues to reverberate throughout the Good Life today.

NOTES

Chapter 1

1. Carlson, Under Cover, 385. For a fascinating, in-depth look into the far-right movements of the 1930s and early 1940s in the United States, see Bradley W. Hart's Hitler's American Friends: The Third Reich's Supporters in the United States (Thomas Dunne Books, 2018).
2. Hurt, Great Plains during World War II.
3. Gallop, "70% Say Aiding Britain Is Best Way," 10.
4. United Press, "Isolationism of Midwest Believed Over-Emphasized."
5. "Nebraska: The Logical Spot."
6. "Here Within Nebraska."
7. "Favors Creation State Defense Committee."
8. Lingeman, Don't You Know There's a War On?
9. "Unicameral: Defense Is Emphasized by Solons."
10. "Defense Committee Group Studies State Capacity for Industry."
11. "Committee on Defense Makes Plans."
12. "New Defense Policy May Aid Nebraska," 10.
13. Ibid., 4.
14. "Asks Chamber of Commerce to Co-Operate 1941," 7
15. Toft, "All Out for Victory," 30.
16. Gilder Lehrman Institute of American History, "Civilian Defense on the Home Front, 1942."
17. Jeffries, Wartime America, 187.

18. "Nebraskans Ready for Defense Responsibility," 3.
19. "Aid in Defense by Saving Waste Paper," 8
20. "Nebraskans Ready for Defense Responsibility."
21. Osborn, "What Did You Do During the War?" 167.
22. Norris, "Norris Quick to Vote."
23. "Lincoln Boys Rush Toward Enlistment."
24. "Students Tense in War Reaction."
25. "Hitler's Hand in Attack Upon Hawaii."
26. "12 Regional Defense Boards Selected."
27. Coe, "Defense Comes Home."
28. "Fast Growing Defense Groups Enroll 2,700."
29. Associated Press, "Civilian Defense Chief Calls All Over 15."
30. "Broadcast for Victory."
31. katiedishman2014, "NARA Coast to Coast."
32. "Gas Rationing."
33. katiedishman2014, "NARA Coast to Coast."
34. "Grant M'Fayden Named as Tire Ration Chief."
35. Associated Press, "Wartime Speed Limit"; "Drivers Asked Go Slower and Save Rubber."
36. "Griswold in New Protest."
37. "Governor Griswold Says Must Be Simpler Manner."
38. Wide World Press, "Business Today: Sugar Rationing."
39. Associated Press, "Teachers Will Issue Sugar Rationing Books."
40. Sarah Sundun, Author, "Make It Do."
41. Stein, "You Don't Need All that Sugar."
42. Hurt, Great Plains during World War II, 133.
43. "Our Country's Crisis in Meat."
44. Associated Press, "Tales of Cattle Rustling Fables."
45. Mason, "Impact of World War II on Women's Fashion."
46. "Law Puts Limit on 5 Gallons of Gas on Premises."

Chapter 2

47. Miller, "National Register of Historic Places."
48. Hurst, "Nebraska Army Air Fields."
49. Otis, "Big Bombers Nest in Nebraska."
50. Hurst, "Nebraska Army Air Fields."
51. Ibid., 130.

52. "McCook Air Base Soldiers Helping in Potato Harvest."
53. Hurt, Great Plains during World War II, 262.
54. U.S. War Department, "Complete Report Covering Construction and Completion."
55. Explore History Nebraska Team, "Ainsworth Army Air Field."
56. "Ainsworth Airfield Now Occupied."
57. "Military Service Organization Holds Meeting, Monday."
58. "Service Men's Dance at City Hall Proves Successful."
59. "News from the Air Base: Dec. 24, 1942."
60. "News from the Air Base: Dec. 31, 1942."
61. "News from the Air Base: Jan. 7, 1943."
62. "News from the Air Base: Aug. 19, 1943."
63. "News from the Air Base: Aug. 19, 1943."
64. Laresen, "Alliance Army Air Base Case," 239–40.
65. Knight Museum Board and Partners, Alliance, Nebraska, 7.
66. Associated Press, "Silver Wings of Alliance Commandant."
67. U.S. Air Force, "Notes on the Earlier History," 29–30.
68. Daw, "History of Alliance Army Air Base, April-May-June 1944."
69. Ibid., 1.
70. Fly Alliance Nebraska, "Army Airfield Base."
71. Mayer, "History of Alliance Army Air Base."
72. Gordon, "Section and Unit Historical Reports."
73. James, "60,000 at Demonstration by Alliance Airborne Force."
74. "Jumping Dog."
75. "Legal Section Historical Report."
76. Ibid.
77. "Historical Report of the Public Relations Section."
78. Rochn, "Interview with 2nd. Lt. James J. Rochs."
79. Daw, "Interview with Captain Edward J. Jewell."
80. Daw, "History of the Alliance Army Air Base," March 1, 1944.
81. "City Willing to Entertain Soldiers Here."
82. "Local Girls Enjoy Dances at Air Base."
83. Daw, "History of Alliance Army Air Base, April-May-June 1944," 17.
84. "Soldiers Need Coat Hangers."
85. Olson, "Activities Promoted by the Special Services Department."
86. Daw, "History of the Alliance Army Air Base," March 1944: Interviews.
87. Ibid.
88. McKone, "State of Discipline."
89. Olson, "Activities Promoted by the Special Services Department."

90. Ibid.

91. Ibid.

92. Markward, "WAC Section Historical Report."

93. Daw, "History of the Alliance Army Air Base," March 1, 1944.

94. Markward, "WAC Section Historical Report."

95. Penry, Nebraska's Fatal Air Crashes of World War II, 31.

96. Ibid., 35–37.

97. Ibid., 73–74.

98. "Army Airfield Base."

99. Priefert, Those Who Flew, 99.

100. Ibid., 72.

101. Jaffe, "History of Special Service Department."

102. "Bruning's Army Air Field Chapel Opens Today."

103. Priefert, Those Who Flew, 73.

104. Penry, Nebraska's Fatal Air Crashes of World War II, 179–82.

105. Ibid., 185.

106. Ibid., 189–94.

107. Ibid., 197–99.

108. Associated Press, "Transport Crash Fatal to 28 Men; 24 from Bruning."

109. Penry, Nebraska's Fatal Air Crashes of World War II, 204.

110. Village of Fairmont, "Fairmont Army Airfield."

111. Ibid.

112. Office of the Historical Officer, "History of the Fairmont Army Airfield," 2.

113. Ibid., 3.

114. Village of Fairmont, "Fairmont Army Airfield."

115. Hartley, "Developments Exceed Predictions of Airport Sponsors."

116. "Lincoln Air Base Hospital Noted for Skill."

117. Butler, "Religious Activities at Base Center in New Chapel."

118. Brown, "Morale Job Widespread in Its Scope."

119. Brown, "Air Base News: June 11, 1943."

120. Yanik, "Off They Went."

121. "Historical Data for Harvard Army Air Field," June 1944, 6.

122. "Historical Data for Harvard Army Air Field," October 1944.

123. Ibid.

124. Historic Kearney, UNK History Department, "About Kearney Army Air Field," https://historickearney.unk.edu/exhibits/show/kearney-goes-to-war/kaaf_intro.

125. UNK History Department, "About Kearney Army Air Field."

126. Ibid.
127. Petersen, "Kearney, Nebraska, and the Kearney Army Air Field," 121.
128. Ibid.
129. Mattson, "City of Kearney, Nebraska."
130. Petersen, "Kearney, Nebraska, and the Kearney Army Air Field," 122.
131. Hurt, Great Plains during World War II, 268.
132. "Urban League Girls Guests Kearney Base."
133. "Notice to All Clark Gable Fans."
134. Associated Press, "Kearney Crash Kills 6 Including Omaha Flier."
135. Ibid., "Injuries Fatal to Seventh Flier in Army Bomber Crash."
136. "WAC Mess Hall Dressed Up with Colorful Paint, Drapes."
137. "D-Day Arrives for WACs at KAAF."
138. Petersen, "Kearney, Nebraska, and the Kearney Army Air Field," 126–27.
139. "War Department Calls for Bids on Air Base."
140. Lincoln Chamber of Commerce, "In Response to the Inspiring Challenge."
141. Gellermann, "Lincoln Army Air Field History," 1.
142. Ibid., 28.
143. Lincoln Air Force Base.
144. Gellermann, "Lincoln Army Air Field History."
145. Ibid.
146. Ibid., 235.
147. "Lincoln Air Base Hospital Noted for Skill."
148. Gellermann, "Lincoln Army Air Field History," 68.
149. Ibid., 72.
150. Ibid., 73.
151. "New USO Club to Open Sunday for Negro Soldiers."
152. "Joe Louis Is Due Next Wednesday."
153. "Narrative History Army Air Field McCook Nebraska," 4.
154. Sehnert, "Norden Bombsight in World War II."
155. "History of McCook Army Air Field 17th Bombardment," 2.
156. Ibid., 3–5.
157. Real-McKeighan, "Base Played Role in Training Nation's Pilots."
158. "Scribner Army Air Field 4316 AAF Base Unit History."
159. "History of Scribner Air Base."
160. Real-McKeighan, "Base Played Role in Training Nation's Pilots."
161. Associated Press, "Four K-9s Help Guard Air Base."
162. "Scribner Army Air Field 4316 AAF Base Unit History."

163. Associated Press, "Scribner Air Field Now 'Standby' Base."
164. "History Army Air Base, Scottsbluff, NE."
165. Ibid.

Chapter 3

166. Buecker, Fort Robinson and the American Century, 77.
167. Ibid., 81–82.
168. Ibid., 84.
169. Amateis, "Fido Goes to War."
170. Buecker, Fort Robinson and the American Century, 93–94.
171. Ibid., 95.
172. Ibid., 96.
173. Amateis, "Fido Goes to War."
174. Gregory, "Handling, Feeding, and Care of War Dogs."
175. "Introductory Notes and Instructions on Training War Dogs," 2.
176. Buecker, Fort Robinson and the American Century, 102–3.
177. "Nebraska Army Post Trains All War Dogs."
178. Amateis, "Fido Goes to War."
179. Buecker, Fort Robinson and the American Century, 105.
180. Ibid., 106.
181. Ibid., 100–101.
182. Amateis, "Fido Goes to War."
183. Buecker, Fort Robinson and the American Century, 131.

Chapter 4

184. "Scrap Shortage."
185. Kimble, Prairie Forge, 26–31.
186. Ibid.
187. Ibid., 32–35.
188. Ibid., 49.
189. Ibid., 48.
190. "Doorly Urges State Lead in Salvage Drive."
191. "Mr. and Mrs. Nebraska Farmer."
192. "Hamlet or City, All Swing into Nebraska Scrap Drive."
193. "U. of N. Cannon to Join Scrap Drive."

194. "Hamlet or City, All Swing into Nebraska Scrap Drive."
195. Morrow, "Scotts Bluffs Drafts Men, Women, Children."
196. O'Hanlon, "Scrap Hunters Will 'Dig Needles from Haystacks.'"
197. "Throngs Expected to Greet Abbott, Costello."
198. "Let's Have It!"
199. United Press, "State Scrap Drive Hits 17 Million Pounds Collection."
200. "'Amazing,' Expert Says of Scrap Drive."
201. "Proclamation: State of Nebraska, Executive Office, Lincoln."
202. Kimble, Prairie Forge, 111.
203. "59,167 Tons New Total for Scrap," 2.
204. Kimble, Prairie Forge, 118.
205. Ibid., 119.
206. "Nebraska to the Rescue."
207. Kimble, Prairie Forge, 135.
208. Pulitzer Prizes, "1943 Pulitzer Prize Winner in Public Service."
209. "Higgins Declares River Is National, Not Local Problem," 8.

Chapter 5

210. Thompson, Prisoners on the Plains, 155.
211. Spencer, "Prisoners of War in Cheyenne County."
212. Thompson, Prisoners on the Plains, 236–37.
213. Buecker, Fort Robinson and the American Century, 124.
214. McNight, "Employment of Prisoners of War," 50.
215. Kruse, "Custody of Prisoners of War," 72.
216. U.S. War Department, 7th Service Command, "Handbook on Facilities of Posts, Camp, and Stations."
217. Krammer, Nazi Prisoners of War in America, 37–38.
218. Thompson, Men in German Uniform, 6.
219. Downie and Stanton, "Italians Taken in Africa War Interned."
220. Hinman, "Personal Recollections of the Scottsbluff POW Camp."
221. "Bridgeport Escapees Are Captured in Colorado."
222. Associated Press, "Scottsbluff War Prisoners Seized."
223. Krammer, Nazi Prisoners of War in America, 180–81.
224. Robin, Barbed-Wire College, 195.
225. Gansberg, Stalag USA, 77.
226. Thompson, "Letters of June 30, 1945 and Feb. 19, 1946." To read more about the Intellectual Diversion Program, see Ron Robin's Barbed-Wire College.

227. For a comprehensive overview of the POW camps in Nebraska, please see my book Nebraska POW Camps: A History of World War II Prisoners in the Heartland (The History Press, 2014).

Chapter 6

228. "Nebraska Sites for Ammunition Depots Studied."
229. Hurt, Great Plains during World War II, 39.
230. Ibid., 60.
231. Associated Press, "War Plant to Grand Island."
232. Ferguson, "Historic Properties Report," 13.
233. Ibid., 20.
234. Ibid., 27.
235. Ibid., 31.
236. McKee, "Cornhusker Ordnance Plants Helped America."
237. Wit, "Social and Economic Impact," 158–59.
238. Ibid., 156–58.
239. Moseley, author interview.
240. Budde, "Looking Back on 1945 Explosion."
241. Stein, "Historical Facts of the Former Nebraska Ordnance Plant."
242. Gustafson, "Farmer's Complaint."
243. Associated Press, "$371,356 Price on 2,949 Acres."
244. "Lincoln Allotted 80 New Housing Units."
245. "More or Less Personal," editorial, Evening State Journal, June 11, 1942.
246. "Farm Workers Urged to Aid in Industries in War Emergency."
247. Stein, "Historical Facts of the Former Nebraska Ordnance Plant."
248. "TNT Poisoning at Mead Is 'Low.'"
249. "Nebraska Goes to War."
250. "2,840,000 Was Mead's Total."
251. Laukaitis, "NU, EPA Reach Deal."
252. Russell, "World War II Boomtown." In her article, Russell discussed the significant impact the depot had on Hastings, focusing in particular on the racial tensions and animosity between new and old residents.
253. "More or Less Personal," editorial, Evening State Journal, June 11, 1942.
254. Adams County Nebraska Historical Society, "Naval Ammunition Depot."
255. Miller, U.S. Naval Ammunition Depot, 13–15.
256. Adams County Nebraska Historical Society, "Spencer Park."

257. Miller, "National Register of Historic Places," 21.
258. Miller, U.S. Naval Ammunition Depot, 38–39.
259. Hurt, Great Plains during World War II, 258.
260. Osborn, "What Did You Do During the War?" 202.
261. Hurt, Great Plains during World War II, 258.
262. Ibid., 259.
263. Hurt, Great Plains during World War II, 260–62.
264. "May Transfer Indians to Hastings Project."
265. Hurt, Great Plains during World War II, 362.
266. Miller, U.S. Naval Ammunition Depot, 100. Miller provided an in-depth view of each explosion and included the Military Court of Inquiry investigation results.
267. Miller, U.S. Naval Ammunition Depot, 111–21.
268. Mahlman, Sioux Army Depot, 3.
269. Ibid., 1.
270. Ibid., 7.
271. Associated Press, "No One Is Idle in Sidney."
272. "Appeal to the People of Sidney."
273. Lowe, "Sidney Bursting at Seams."
274. Mahlman, Sioux Army Depot, 5–6.
275. Ibid., 10.
276. Ibid., 18.
277. Ibid., 19.
278. Associated Press, "Italian Captives at Sioux Depot."
279. Ibid., "Sioux Ordnance Depot Will Use Japanese Labor."
280. Mahlman, Sioux Army Depot, 28.
281. Ibid., 189.
282. "Summary of the Productive Operation of the Glenn L. Martin–Nebraska Company."
283. United Press, "Contracts for Bomber Plant at Omaha Signed."
284. Larson, "Nebraska's World War II Bomber Plant," 34.
285. "Summary of the Productive Operation of the Glenn L. Martin–Nebraska Company."
286. Larson, "Nebraska's World War II Bomber Plant," 35.
287. "Summary of the Productive Operation of the Glenn L. Martin–Nebraska Company."
288. "Brief Description of Testing Program."
289. Larson, "Nebraska's World War II Bomber Plant," 38–39.
290. "Introduction and Tour Preparation Talk," 6.

291. Associated Press, "Private Housing in Nebraska in '44."
292. "Midwest Production Impresses Roosevelt."
293. Boeing, "Historical Snapshot: B-29 Superfortress."
294. Air Force Association, "Smithsonian and the Enola Gay."
295. Penry, Nebraska's Fatal Air Crashes of World War II, 11–13.
296. Ibid., 69–70.
297. Ibid., 70–71.
298. Larson, "Nebraska's World War II Bomber Plant."

Chapter 7

299. Greene, Once Upon a Town, 14–15.
300. Reisdorff, North Platte Canteen, 9–11.
301. Norton, "Catering to the Troops," 37.
302. Ibid., 41–42.
303. Greene, Once Upon a Town, 72.
304. Hinman, "Nebraska Women in the War," 124.
305. Ibid., 127.
306. Norton, "Catering to the Troops," 46.
307. Lincoln County Historical Museum, "The North Platte Canteen."
308. Norton, "Catering to the Troops," 47–50.
309. Universal Press, "Platte Lad Sells Shirts for Canteen."
310. Norton, "Catering to the Troops," 54–55.
311. United Press, "Lad Gets $5 from Letter to President."
312. Lincoln County Historical Museum, "The North Platte Canteen."
313. Norton, "Catering to the Troops," 80–81.
314. Ibid.
315. Associated Press, "North Platte Canteen Should Continue."
316. Ibid., "Over 7,000 Servicemen Treated to Christmas."

Chapter 8

317. Ayling, Calling All Women, 151.
318. Ibid., 152.
319. Yellin, Our Mothers' War, 167.
320. "County Quota Cards, Morrill County and Scotts Bluff County."
321. "U.S.O. Coming to Lincoln."

322. "Lincoln USO Headquarters Off to a Head Start."
323. "Lincoln Extends 'Welcome' to Service Men, Women."
324. "Scottsbluff Citizens Rally to Provide Service Center."
325. "Welcome Sign Out at Hebron USO."
326. "Donations to Center."
327. "Public Invited to Ceremony Sunday."
328. "Canteen Feed for Internees."
329. "Organization and Standards."
330. Nelson, "Morale-Builders the Lincolnettes."
331. "Lincolnettes: Rules and Instructions."
332. Gordon, "Mary Gordon Column."
333. Gordon, "Mary Gordon Column June 27."
334. Yellin, Our Mothers' War, 131.
335. "Minerva's Mail."
336. "Officers Stationed in Lincoln Enjoy Dances."

Chapter 9

337. Lukesh, Lucky Ears, 46.
338. "Ben Kuroki, American."
339. Associated Press, "Nebraska Japs 'Loneliest Boys' in American Army."
340. Kubota, Most Honorable Son.
341. Lukesh, Lucky Ears, 62.
342. Stewart, "Ben Kuroki's 59th Mission." Although Kuroki did not have any formal training, he had practiced on his own. According to Sam McGowan, this was not unusual. He wrote, "In 1942, the Army Air Forces were in their infancy, and no training program had been developed for aerial gunners. Pilots had the option of picking their own enlisted crew members from among squadron ground personnel, and Ben was constantly pressing for aircrew duty. Most enlisted aircrew members had been trained in skills directly related to aircraft and systems maintenance or were trained as radio operators, but the need for aerial gunners allowed pilots to choose whomever they wanted as a replacement when there was a vacancy on their crew." See McGowan, "Bomber Gunner Ben Kuroki," at https://warfarehistorynetwork.com/daily/wwii/bomber-gunner-ben-kuroki-most-honorable-son.
343. Martin, Boy from Nebraska, 87.
344. Lukesh, Lucky Ears, 66–67.

345. McGowan, "Bomber Gunner Ben Kuroki."
346. Lukesh, Lucky Ears, 69–72.
347. National World War II Museum, Ben Kuroki.
348. McGowan, "Bomber Gunner Ben Kuroki."
349. National World War II Museum, Ben Kuroki.
350. Boyne, "Tidal Wave."
351. Cronkite, "Nebraska Jap on Liberator Is 'Fightingist.'"
352. McGowan, "Bomber Gunner Ben Kuroki."
353. Lukesh, Lucky Ears, 78.
354. Martin, Boy from Nebraska, 158.
355. Lukesh, Lucky Ears, 83.
356. Cronkite, "Nebraska Jap on Liberator Is 'Fightingist.'"
357. tenBroek, Barnhart and Matson, Prejudice, War, and the Constitution, 19.
358. Ibid., 24.
359. Ibid., 68.
360. National World War II Museum, Ben Kuroki.
361. Lukesh, Lucky Ears, 88.
362. National World War II Museum, Ben Kuroki.
363. Ibid.
364. Martin, Boy from Nebraska, 173–74.
365. Ibid., 174.
366. Tysver, "Kuroki Beat Bias to Serve with Distinction."
367. Martin, Boy from Nebraska, 175–76.
368. "Nisei Gunner 'Takes Care.'"
369. National World War II Museum, Ben Kuroki.
370. Stewart, "Ben Kuroki's 59th Mission."
371. "Ben Kuroki, Nisei War Hero." It is also worth noting that the University of Nebraska accepted about one hundred Nisei students from internment camps between 1942 and 1945 during a time when many universities and colleges refused. See UNL's Nisei collection, http://unlhistory.unl.edu/exhibits/show/nisei/nisei-experience-at-unl.
372. Lukesh, Lucky Ears, 111–13.
373. Ibid., 114–16.
374. Strahan, Andrew Jackson Higgins, 6.
375. Ibid., 4–8.
376. Ibid., 21–22.
377. Brinkley, "Man Who Won the War for Us."
378. Strahan, Andrew Jackson Higgins, 20.
379. Burck, "Mr. Higgins and His Wonderful Boats."

380. Strahan, Andrew Jackson Higgins, 24.
381. Ibid., 88.
382. Brinkley, "Man Who Won the War for Us."
383. Ibid.
384. National World War II Museum, "Research Starters: Higgins Boats."
385. Sidey, "Home Front."
386. Strahan, Andrew Jackson Higgins, 222.
387. Ibid., 238.
388. Ibid., 224–25.
389. Ibid., 264.
390. Ibid., 315.
391. Ibid., 341.
392. Higgins Memorial Project.

Chapter 10

393. Amateis, "Enough Food to Feed an Army."
394. "Hold the Farms or Lose the War."
395. Hurt, Great Plains during World War II, 179.
396. Amateis, "Enough Food to Feed an Army."
397. Hurt, Great Plains during World War II, 188.

BIBLIOGRAPHY

Adams County Nebraska Historical Society. "The Naval Ammunition Depot." www.adamshistory.org.

———. "Spencer Park." www.adamshistory.org.

"Aid in Defense by Saving Waste Paper, Rubber, and Metals." Lincoln Star, November 12, 1941.

"Ainsworth Airfield Now Occupied." Ainsworth Star-Journal, December 17, 1942.

Air Force Association. "The Smithsonian and the Enola Gay." Air Force Magazine. www.airforcemag.com.

Amateis, Melissa A. "Enough Food to Feed an Army: How Farmers Kept the GIs Fighting." America in World War II (October 2013).

———. "Fido Goes to War: The War Dogs of World War II." America in World War II (April 2015).

"'Amazing,' Expert Says of Scrap Drive." Omaha World-Herald, July 30, 1942.

"An Appeal to the People of Sidney." Editorial, Sidney Telegraph, March 20, 1942.

"Asks Chamber of Commerce to Cooperate." Evening State Journal, May 14, 1941.

Associated Press. "Buying Land for Sidney War Plant." Evening State Journal, March 21, 1942.

———. "Civilian Defense Chief Calls All Over 15 to Volunteer Services." Lincoln Star, January 4, 1942.

———. "Four K-9s Help Guard Air Base." Lincoln Journal Star, November 5, 1943.

———. "Injuries Fatal to Seventh Flier in Army Bomber Crash." Lincoln Star, February 11, 1944.

———. "Italian Captives at Sioux Depot." Lincoln Journal Star, January 24, 1944, Main edition.

———. "Kearney Crash Kills 6 Including Omaha Flier." Lincoln Star, February 2, 1944.

———. "Nebraska Japs 'Loneliest Boys' in American Army." Lincoln Star, February 5, 1944.

———. "'No One Is Idle in Sidney': Ordnance Depot Attracts Workers; Community About to 'Burst Its Seams.'" Omaha World-Herald, June 7, 1942.

———. "North Platte Canteen Should Continue—Jeffers." Lincoln Journal Star, December 11, 1945.

———. "Over 7,000 Servicemen Treated to Christmas Cheer by Canteen." Lincoln Journal Star, December 26, 1945.

———. "Private Housing in Nebraska in '44 Showed Common Sense Trend—Holm." Nebraska State Journal, December 24, 1944.

———. "Scottsbluff War Prisoners Seized." Nebraska State Journal, November 13, 1944.

———. "Scribner Air Field Now 'Standby' Base." Lincoln Star, March 4, 1944.

———. "Silver Wings of Alliance Commandant Observing Their Silver Anniversary." Lincoln Star, September 2, 1942.

———. "Sioux Ordnance Depot Will Use Japanese Labor." Lincoln Star, September 18, 1944.

———. "Tales of Cattle Rustling Fables." Lincoln Star, February 27, 1943, 1.

———. "Teachers Will Issue Sugar Rationing Books; Urged to 'Crack Down' on Hoarders." Nebraska State Journal, February 7, 1942.

———. "$371,356 Price on 2,949 Acres." Omaha World-Herald, September 15, 1944.

———. "Transport Crash Fatal to 28 Men; 24 from Bruning. Plunge Near Naper; May Have Been Storm Victim." Evening State Journal, August 4, 1944.

———. "War Plant to Grand Island: Ordnance Plant to Be Named the Cornhusker." Evening State Journal, February 13, 1942.

———. "War Plant Workers Cause Problem of Children's Welfare." Lincoln Journal Star, June 5, 1943.

———. "Wartime Speed Limit of 35 Miles an Hour Placed in Effect Today…Enforcement Methods Vary." Lincoln Star, October 1, 1942.

Ayling, Keith. Calling All Women: The American Women's Guide to Voluntary Service. New York: Harper, 1942.

"Ben Kuroki, American." TIME (February 7, 1944).

"Ben Kuroki, Nisei War Hero, Now G.I. Freshman at U. of N." Lincoln Journal Star, June 24, 1947.

Boeing. "Historical Snapshot: B-29 Superfortress." Boeing, blog. https://www.boeing.com.

Boyne, Walter J. "Tidal Wave." Air Force Magazine (December 2007). http://www.airforcemag.com.

"Bridgeport Escapees Are Captured in Colorado." Lincoln Star, July 9, 1945.

"Brief Description of Testing Program." N.d. MS0366: Martin Bomber Plant, History Nebraska.

Brinkley, Douglas. "The Man Who Won the War for Us." American Heritage, June 2000. https://www.americanheritage.com.

"Broadcast for Victory." Lincoln Star, July 26, 1942.

Brown, Corporal Irving L. "Air Base News: June 11, 1943." Grand Island Independent, June 11, 1943.

———. "Morale Job Widespread in Its Scope." Grand Island Independent, June 11, 1943.

"Bruning's Army Air Field Chapel Opens Today." Nebraska State Journal, July 25, 1943.

Budde, Gene. "Looking Back on 1945 Explosion." Grand Island Independent, June 6, 2005.

Buecker, Thomas R. Fort Robinson and the American Century: 1900–1948. Norman: University of Oklahoma Press, 2002.

Burck, Gilbert. "Mr. Higgins and His Wonderful Boats." LIFE (August 16, 1943).

Butler, Sergeant Irving. "Religious Activities at Base Center in New Chapel: Much Like Quaint County Churches Found in Vermont." Grand Island Independent, June 11, 1943.

Callahan, Bill. "Fairmont Army Airfield." National Register of Historic Places, October 22, 2002.

"Canteen Feed for Internees." Omaha World-Herald, May 27, 1945, Sunday edition, sec. 5-E.

Carlson, John Roy. Under Cover: My Four Years in the Nazi Underworld of America. New York: E.P. Dutton & Company Inc., 1943.

"City Willing to Entertain Soldiers Here: Interviews Show People Are Ready to Go Ahead If USO Fails to Act." Alliance Times-Herald, November 17, 1942.

Coe, Lula Mae. "Defense Comes Home." Lincoln Star, December 14, 1941.

"Committee on Defense Makes Plans." Evening State Journal, February 25, 1941.

"County Quota Cards, Morrill County and Scotts Bluff County." 1942. RG1331.AM, Series 1—Correspondence, 1942–1946, History Nebraska.

Cowan, J. Harold. "It's Called 'Biggest Ammunition Depot in the World.'" Omaha World-Herald, July 4, 1943, Omaha World-Herald Magazine edition, sec. 12-C.

Cronkite, Walter. "Nebraska Jap on Liberator Is 'Fightingist.'" Lincoln Star, November 11, 1943.

Daw, Sergeant Joseph W. "History of Alliance Army Air Base, April-May-June 1944." June 1944. RG538, Series 3, roll no. 4, History Nebraska.

———. "History of the Alliance Army Air Base." March 1, 1944. RG538, roll no. 3, B2004, History Nebraska.

———. "History of the Alliance Army Air Base." March 1944: Interviews. RG538, roll no. 3, B2004, History Nebraska.

———. "Interview with Captain Edward J. Jewell." March 9, 1944. RG538, roll no. 3, B2004, History Nebraska.

"D-Day Arrives for WACs at KAAF." The Duster 2, no. 17 (July 28, 1944).

"Defense Committee Group Studies State Capacity for Industry." Nebraska State Journal, February 25, 1941.

"Donations to Center." Omaha World-Herald, July 23, 1944, Sunday edition.

"Doorly Urges State Lead in Salvage Drive: Publishing Points Out Critical Necessity for Vital Material." Omaha World-Herald, July 12, 1942, Sunday World-Herald edition, sec. A.

Downie, M.W., and Doug Stanton. "Italians Taken in Africa War Interned at Scottsbluff Camp." Star-Herald, June 25, 1943.

"Drivers Asked Go Slower and Save Rubber." Lincoln Star, January 11, 1942.

Explore History Nebraska Team. "Ainsworth Army Air Field." History Nebraska, October 2019. https://mynehistory.com.

"Fairmont Army Air Field News." U.S. Army Air Corps, June 3, 1944. RG538, Series 5, roll no. 7, History Nebraska.

Fairmont Army Air Field Office of the Historical Officer. "Fairmont Army Air Field History August 1944." U.S. Army Air Corps, August 1944. RG538, Series 5, roll no. 7, History Nebraska.

"Farm Workers Urged to Aid in Industries in War Emergency." Lincoln Star, August 22, 1944.

"Fast Growing Defense Groups Enroll 2,700." Lincoln Star, January 17, 1942.

"Favors Creation State Defense Committee." Lincoln Star, January 27, 1941.

Ferguson, Robert. "Historic Properties Report: Cornhusker Army Munition Plant, Grand Island, Nebraska." Historic Properties Surveys. U.S. Department of the Interior, August 1984. Library of Congress.

"59,167 Tons New Total for Scrap." Omaha World-Herald, August 11, 1942, Morning edition.

Fly Alliance Nebraska. "Army Airfield Base." 2017. http://www.flyalliancene.com.

Fort Robinson POW Camp Headquarters. "Memoir to Headquarters RE: Transfer of Prisoner of War, July 12, 1944." July 12, 1944. Provost Marshal General Documents, Fort Robinson Museum.

Fugate, Tally. "War Production Board." Encyclopedia of Oklahoma History and Culture. https://www.okhistory.org.

Gallop, George. "70% Say Aiding Britain Is Best Way to 'Keep U.S. Out.'" Omaha World-Herald, February 21, 1941.

Gansberg, Judith. Stalag USA: The Remarkable Story of German POWs in America. New York: Thomas Y. Crowell, 1977.

"Gas Rationing: Supply of Basic Books Received by Nebraska OPA to Being Dec. 1." Lincoln Star, November 11, 1942.

Gellermann, Joseph E. "Lincoln Army Air Field History, Dec. 1, 1943." U.S. Army Air Corps, December 1, 1943. RG538, USAF, roll no. 16, History Nebraska.

Gilder Lehrman Institute of American History. "Civilian Defense on the Home Front, 1942." https://www.gilderlehrman.org.

Golden Spike Tower and Visitor Center. "North Platte Canteen." 2017. https://goldenspiketower.com.

"Gold, McCulla Find Lincoln Set as One of USDA Regional Offices." Nebraska State Journal, July 8, 1941.

Gordon, Dudley W. "Section and Unit Historical Reports." 537th Service Squadron. Alliance, Nebraska: U.S. Army Air Corps, March 15, 1944. RG538, roll no. 3, B2004, History Nebraska.

Gordon, Mary. "Mary Gordon Column." Lincoln Star, June 20, 1943.

———. "Mary Gordon Column June 27." Nebraska State Journal, June 27, 1943.

"Governor Griswold Says Must Be Simpler Manner to Curb Pleasure Driving." Lincoln Star, December 1, 1942.

"Grant M'Fayden Named as Tire Ration Chief for Nebraska." Lincoln Star, December 20, 1941.

Greene, Bob. Once Upon a Town: The Miracle of the North Platte Canteen. New York: HarperCollins, 2002.

Gregory, E.B. "Handling, Feeding, and Care of War Dogs; Circular Letter #415." Office of the Quartermaster, U.S. War Department, November 19, 1943. RG1517, Box 11, History Nebraska.

"Griswold in New Protest: Wires Anderson on Gas Ration." Evening State Journal, November 25, 1942.

Gustafson, John. "A Farmer's Complaint." Lincoln Journal Star, December 28, 1943.

"Hamlet or City, All Swing into Nebraska Scrap Drive." Omaha World-Herald, July 25, 1942.

Hartley, Charles L. "Developments Exceed Predictions of Airport Sponsors." Grand Island Independent, June 11, 1943.

"Here Within Nebraska." Editorial, Lincoln Star, July 10, 1940.

"Higgins Declares River Is National, Not Local Problem." Omaha World-Herald, May 13, 1943.

Higgins Memorial Project. http://www.higginsmemorial.com/project.asp.

Hinman, Daisy. "Nebraska Women in the War, in the Service Clubs: The North Platte Canteen." Nebraska History 25 (1944): 124–28.

Hinman, Herb. "Personal Recollections of the Scottsbluff POW Camp." Joe Fairfield Papers, undated. Legacy of the Plains Museum.

"Historical Data for Harvard Army Air Field." U.S. Army Air Corps, June 1944. RG538, roll no. 10, History Nebraska.

"Historical Data for Harvard Army Air Field." U.S. Army Air Corps, October 1944. RG538, roll no. 10, History Nebraska.

"Historical Data for Harvard Army Air Field." U.S. Army Air Corps, September 1943. RG538, roll no. 10, History Nebraska.

"Historical Report of the Public Relations Section." Unit Historical Reports. Alliance, Nebraska, U.S. Army Air Corps, March 11, 1944. RG538, roll no. 3, B2004, History Nebraska.

"History Army Air Base, Scottsbluff, NE." January 1943. RG538, Series 11, roll no. 27, History Nebraska.

"History of McCook Army Air Field 17th Bombardment Operational Wing Second Air Force." U.S. Army Air Corps, February 1945. USAF. RG538, roll no. 19, History Nebraska.

"History of Scribner Air Base, December 1932–December 1943." U.S. Army Air Corps, January 1944. RG538, roll no. 28, Series 12, History Nebraska.

"Hitler's Hand in Attack Upon Hawaii." Editorial, Lincoln Star, December 8, 1941.

"Hold the Farms or Lose the War." Editorial, Alliance Times-Herald, December 8, 1942.

"Home Is Where the Heart Is." Editorial, Omaha World-Herald, November 28, 1944.

Hurst, Robert. "Nebraska Army Air Fields: A Pictorial Review." Nebraska History 76 (1995): 129–43.

Hurt, R. Douglas. The Great Plains during World War II. Lincoln: University of Nebraska Press, 2008.

"Introduction and Tour Preparation Talk." N.d. MS0366: Martin Bomber Plant, History Nebraska.

"Introductory Notes and Instructions on Training War Dogs." May 13, 1943. RG1517, Box 11, History Nebraska.

Jaffe, Sam. "History of Special Service Department, Bruning Army Air Field, November 1942–October 1943." Bruning, Nebraska, U.S. Army Air Corps, October 1943. RG538, roll no. 5, History Nebraska.

James, Burt. "60,000 at Demonstration by Alliance Airborne Force." Lincoln Star, August 23, 1943.

Jeffries, John W. Wartime America: The World War II Home Front. The American Ways Series. Chicago: Ivan R. Dee Publishers, 1996.

"Joe Louis Is Due Next Wednesday: Heavyweight Champ to Perform at Base." Lincoln Sunday Journal and Star, October 10, 1943, sec. 3-B.

"Jumping Dog: Geronimo Is Mascot of 507th Parachute Infantry." LIFE (September 13, 1943).

"Jury Drawn in Land Case: All Mead Plant Area Is Involved." Evening State Journal, August 21, 1944.

katiedishman2014. "NARA Coast to Coast: The Coupon Craze of the 1940s." NARAtions, December 19, 2011. https://narations.blogs.archives.gov.

Kimble, James J. Prairie Forge: The Extraordinary Story of the Nebraska Scrap Metal Drive of World War II. Lincoln: University of Nebraska Press, 2014.

Knight Museum Board and Partners. Alliance, Nebraska. Images of America. Charleston, SC: Arcadia Publishing, 2000.

Krammer, Arnold. Nazi Prisoners of War in America. Lanham, MD: Scarborough House, 1979.

Kruse, Arthur. "Custody of Prisoners of War in the United States." Military Affairs 40, no. 2 (n.d.).

Kubota, Bill. Most Honorable Son. DVD. A production of KDN Films, co-produced with NET Television and the Independent Television Service, 2007.

Laresen, Lawrence. "The Alliance Army Air Base Case." Nebraska History 67 (1986): 239–55.

Larson, George A. "Nebraska's World War II Bomber Plant: The Glenn L. Martin–Nebraska Company." Nebraska History 74 (1993): 32–43.

Laukaitis, Algis. "NU, EPA Reach Deal Over More Cleanup at Former Ordnance Plant." Lincoln Journal Star, January 7, 2015.

"Law Puts Limit on 5 Gallons of Gas on Premises." Lincoln Star, December 1, 1942.

"Legal Section Historical Report." Alliance, Nebraska, U.S. Army Air Corps, March 1944. USAF. RG538, Series 3, roll no. 3, B2004, Historical Reports, History Nebraska.

"'Let's Have It!' Cry Abbott, Costello in Drive for Scrap." Evening World-Herald, July 31, 1942.

"Letter to K.B. Clary from C. N. Philbrick (June 28, 1942); Letter to C.N. Philbrick from K.B. Clary (June 30, 1942)." N.d., RG1331.AM, Series 1—Correspondence, 1942–1946, History Nebraska.

"Lincoln Air Base Hospital Noted for Skill of Its Doctors." Nebraska State Journal, March 31, 1943, sec. Editorial.

Lincoln Air Force Base. https://ipfs.io/ipfs/QmXoypizjW3WknFiJnKLw HCnL72vedxjQkDDP1mXWo6uco/wiki/Lincoln_Air_Force_Base.html.

"Lincoln Allotted 80 New Housing Units." Lincoln Star, March 23, 1943.

"Lincoln Boys Rush Toward Enlistment." Evening State Journal, December 8, 1941.

Lincoln Chamber of Commerce. "In Response to the Inspiring Challenge of Colonel Early E.W. Duncan." Lincoln Sunday Journal and Star, May 17, 1942.

"Lincoln Contractors Submit Lowest Bid for New Air Base." Nebraska State Journal, April 9, 1942.

Lincoln County Historical Museum. "The North Platte Canteen." 2012.

"Lincolnette Colonels Campaign Against Loneliness for Soldiers." Lincoln Star, July 23, 1944.

"Lincolnettes: Rules and Instructions." N.d. RG1182.AM: Lincolnettes, History Nebraska.

"Lincoln Extends 'Welcome' to Service Men, Women." Nebraska State Journal, October 10, 1943.

"Lincoln USO Headquarters Off to a Head Start." Lincoln Sunday Journal and Star, October 11, 1942, sec. D.

Lingeman, Richard R. Don't You Know There's a War On?: American Homefront, 1941–1945. New York: G.P. Putnam Sons, 1971.

"Local Girls Enjoy Dances at Air Base." Alliance Times-Herald, November 17, 1942.

"Local USO Prospects Encourage Air Base Soldiers to Air Ideas." Lincoln Sunday Journal and Star, July 26, 1942.

Lowe, Jack. "Sidney Bursting at Seams as War Workers Pour into State's Newest 'Boom Town.'" Lincoln Star, July 31, 1942.

Lukesh, Jean A. "Kuroki, Ben." American National Biography, February 15, 2018. http://www.anb.org.

———. Lucky Ears: The True Story of Ben Kuroki, World War II Hero. Grand Island, NE: Field Mouse Productions, 2010.

Mahlman, Larry L. Sioux Army Depot, 1942–1967. Sidney, NE: Department of the Army, 1966.

Markward, Ellen L. "WAC Section Historical Report." Unit Historical Reports. Alliance, Nebraska, U.S. Army Air Corps, March 1944. USAF. RG538, roll no. 3, B2004, History Nebraska.

Martin, Ralph G. Boy from Nebraska: The Story of Ben Kuroki. New York: Harper and Brothers, 1946.

Mason, Meghann. "The Impact of World War II on Women's Fashion in the United States and Britain." Dissertation, University of Nevada, 2011. https://digitalscholarship.unlv.edu.

Mattson, Ivan. "City of Kearney, Nebraska." Kearney Air Base News 1, no., 1 (April 9, 1943).

Mayer, Second Lieutenant (WAC) Mary. "History of Alliance Army Air Base: Report #5: Civilian Personnel." March 15, 1944. RG538, Series 3, roll no. 3, History Nebraska.

"May Transfer Indians to Hastings Project." Alliance Times-Herald, December 25, 1942.

"McCook Air Base Soldiers Helping in Potato Harvest." Lincoln Star, September 13, 1943.

McGowan, Sam. "Bomber Gunner Ben Kuroki: 'Most Honorable Son.'" Warfare History Network, blog, November 28, 2018. https://warfarehistorynetwork.com.

McKee, Jim. "Cornhusker Ordnance Plants Helped America Win WWII." Lincoln Journal Star, January 12, 2014.

McKinney, T/5 William C. "Hospital at Base Rated with Best." Grand Island Independent, June 11, 1943.

McKone, John V. "State of Discipline, 507th Parachute Infantry, Base Intelligence Office." June 24, 1943. RG538, roll no. 3, B2004, History Nebraska.

McNight, Major Maxwell S. "The Employment of Prisoners of War in the United States." International Labour Review 50, no. 1 (July 1944).

"Mead Ordnance Plant Is 90 Percent Done, Strawn Says." Nebraska State Journal, September 24, 1942.

"Midwest Production Impresses Roosevelt." Lincoln Star, April 24, 1943.

"Military Service Organization Holds Meeting, Monday." Ainsworth Star-Journal, November 5, 1942.

Miller, Greg. "National Register of Historic Places Multiple Property Documentation Form: Relic Components of Army Air Fields in Nebraska." U.S. Department of the Interior, National Park Service, May 18, 1993.

Miller, Walter L. U.S. Naval Ammunition Depot: Hastings, Nebraska, U.S.A. N.p.: self-published, 2013.

"Minerva's Mail: Take Your Thoughts to Minerva." Lincoln Star, July 20, 1942.

"More or Less Personal." Editorial, Evening State Journal, June 11, 1942.

"More or Less Personal." Editorial, Lincoln Sunday Journal and Star, August 9, 1942.

"'More or Less Personal': State Journal Editorial Notes." Evening State Journal, August 29, 1942.

Morrow, Lettie. "Scotts Bluffs Drafts Men, Women, Children." Omaha World-Herald, July 24, 1942.

Moseley, Ellamae. Author interview, November 2, 2017.

"Mr. and Mrs. Nebraska Farmer: It's Up to YOU to Set the Pace for All America!" Ad, Omaha World-Herald, July 30, 1942, Morning World-Herald edition.

"Narrative History Army Air Field McCook Nebraska." U.S. Army Air Corps, April 1944. USAF. RG538, roll no. 18, History Nebraska.

National World War II Museum. Ben Kuroki, 2015. National World War II Museum, New Orleans. https://www.ww2online.org.

———. "Research Starters: Higgins Boats." https://www.nationalww2museum. org.

"Nebraska Army Post Trains All War Dogs." Lincoln Star, June 17, 1945, sec. Sunday Journal and Star Feature.

"Nebraska Goes to War: Bombs for Hitler, Hirohito Loaded at Grand Island." Omaha World-Herald Magazine (July 4, 1943).

"Nebraskans Ready for Defense Responsibility." Lincoln Star, October 28, 1941.

"Nebraska Sites for Ammunition Depots Studied." Lincoln Star, November 11, 1941.

"Nebraska: The Logical Spot for Defense Industry 1940." Ad, Lincoln Star, July 7, 1940.

"Nebraska to the Rescue." LIFE (September 21, 1942).

Nelson, Winn. "Morale-Builders the Lincolnettes." Lincoln Star, August 9, 1942.

"New Defense Policy May Aid Nebraska." Nebraska State Journal, April 1, 1941.

"News from the Air Base: Aug. 19, 1943." Ainsworth Star-Journal, August 19, 1943.

"News from the Air Base: Dec. 31, 1942." Ainsworth Star-Journal, December 31, 1942.

"News from the Air Base: Dec. 24, 1942." Ainsworth Star-Journal, December 24, 1942.

"News from the Air Base: Jan. 7, 1943." Ainsworth Star-Journal, January 7, 1943.

"New USO Club to Open Sunday for Negro Soldiers." Lincoln Sunday Journal and Star, October 10, 1943.

"Nisei Gunner 'Takes Care.'" Omaha World-Herald, February 25, 1945, Sunday World-Herald edition.

Norris, George. "Norris Quick to Vote for War on Japan." Evening State Journal, December 8, 1941.

Norton, Matthew. "Catering to the Troops: The North Platte Canteen and the Myth, Memory, and Legend of the Good War." Master's thesis, University of Nebraska at Kearney, 2014.

"Notables Here to Attend Air Base Opening." Grand Island Independent, June 11, 1943.

"Notice to All Clark Gable Fans—Address Letters to Kearney, Nebraska." Lincoln Star, April 8, 1943.

Office of the Historical Officer. "History of the Fairmont Army Airfield May 1944." U.S. Army Air Corps, May 1944. RG538, roll no. 7, History Nebraska.

"Officers Stationed in Lincoln Enjoy Dances the Lincolnette Organization Is Sponsoring." Lincoln Star, August 6, 1944.

O'Hanlon, Reed, Jr. "Scrap Hunters Will 'Dig Needles from Haystacks.'" Omaha World-Herald, July 18, 1942, Morning World-Herald edition.

Olson, Earl H. "Activities Promoted by the Special Services Department from Date of Base Activation through February 1944." Alliance, Nebraska, U.S. Army Air Corps, March 13, 1944. USAF, RG538, Series 3, B2004, Historical Reports, History Nebraska.

"Organization and Standards." N.d. RG1182.AM: Lincolnettes, History Nebraska.

Osborn, Robert. "What Did You Do During the War?" Nebraska History 72, no. 4 (Winter 1991): 167.

Otis, Howard J. "Big Bombers Nest in Nebraska." Omaha World-Herald, July 4, 1943, sec. Sunday World-Herald Magazine.

"Our Country's Crisis in Meat." Ad, Lincoln Star, March 18, 1943.

Padmore, George. "Japanese Flyer from Nebraska Is First Non-White in U.S. Air Corps in Britain." Chicago Defender, March 5, 1943, National edition.

Penry, Jerry. Nebraska's Fatal Air Crashes of World War II. Milford, NE: Blue Mound Press, 2009.

Petersen, Todd L. "Kearney, Nebraska, and the Kearney Army Air Field in World War II." Nebraska History 72 (1991): 118–26.

Priefert, Virginia. Those Who Flew. Paducah, KY: Turner Publishing Company, 2002.

"Proclamation: State of Nebraska, Executive Office, Lincoln." Omaha World-Herald, August 5, 1942.

"Public Invited to Ceremony Sunday—Citation to Service Enter." Omaha World-Herald, December 26, 1943, Sunday edition.

The Pulitzer Prizes. "The 1943 Pulitzer Prize Winner in Public Service." https://www.pulitzer.org.

Raymond, Jack. "Letter to Frank Finley." December 30, 1942. RG1331. AM, Series 1—Correspondence, 1942–1946, History Nebraska.

Real-McKeighan, Tammy. "Base Played Role in Training Nation's Pilots." Fremont Tribune, August 27, 2011.

Reed, R.W. "How to Land Troops in Europe." Omaha World-Herald Magazine, n.d., sec. 8-C.

Reisdorff, James J. North Platte Canteen: An Account of Heartland Hospitality Along the Union Pacific Railroad. 8th printing. North Platte, NE: North Platte Lincoln County Convention and Visitors Bureau, 2013.

Robin, Ron. The Barbed-Wire College: Reeducating German POWs in the United States during World War II. Princeton, NJ: Princeton University Press, 1995.

Rochn, James J. "Interview with 2nd. Lt. James J. Rochs Acting Base S-2, Pertaining to Relations with the Civilian Population of Alliance." March 1944. RG538, roll no. 3, B2004, History Nebraska.

"Rosalie Lippincott on the North Platte Canteen." YouTube. Hall County Nebraska Historical Society, 2011. https://www.youtube.com.

Russell, Beverly. "World War II Boomtown: Hastings and the Naval Ammunition Depot." Nebraska History 76 (1995): 75–83.

Sarah Sundun, Author. "Make It Do—Sugar Rationing in World War II." http://www.sarahsundin.com.

"Scottsbluff Citizens Rally to Provide Service Center." Omaha World-Herald, July 9, 1943.

"Scrap Shortage: A Problem in Steel Operations." Scientific American, December 1941.

"Scribner Army Air Field 4316 AAF Base Unit History." U.S. Army Air Corps, January 1945. RG538, roll no. 28, History Nebraska.

Sehnert, Walt. "The Norden Bombsight in World War II." McCook Gazette, March 23, 2009.

"Service Men's Dance at City Hall Proves Successful." Ainsworth Star-Journal, December 24, 1942.

"Sgt. Kuroki Returns from Pacific Duty." Omaha World-Herald, November 8, 1945.

Sidey, Hugh. "The Home Front." TIME (June 13, 1994).

"Soldiers Need Coat Hangers." Alliance Times-Herald, October 20, 1942.

"A Soldier's Tribute: 'Always Room for Strangers at the North Platte Canteen.'" Omaha World-Herald, January 27, 1944, Morning edition.

Spencer, Ralph. "Prisoners of War in Cheyenne County, 1943–1946." Nebraska History 63, no. 3 (1982): 438–49.

Stein, David A. "You Don't Need All that Sugar." Lincoln Sunday Journal and Star, April 26, 1942.

Stein, Kristine. "Historical Facts of the Former Nebraska Ordnance Plant." U.S. Army Corps of Engineers, Kansas City District, n.d. https://usace.contentdm.oclc.org.

Stewart, Cal W. "Ben Kuroki's 59th Mission." Omaha World-Herald, n.d. Sunday World-Herald Magazine edition.

Strahan, Jerry. Andrew Jackson Higgins and the Boats that Won World War II. Baton Rouge: Louisiana State University Press, 1994.

"Students Tense in War Reaction." Daily Nebraskan, December 8, 1941.

"Summary of the Productive Operation of the Glenn L. Martin–Nebraska Company." Glenn L. Martin Company, n.d. RG 3817.AM, MS 0366, S1 B1.F2, History Nebraska.

tenBroek, Jacobus, Edward N. Barnhart and Floyd W. Matson. Prejudice, War, and the Constitution. 3rd printing. Berkeley: University of California Press, 1968.

Thompson, Alfred. "Letters of June 30, 1945 and Feb. 19, 1946." June 30, 1945. Fort Robinson Museum.

Thompson, Antonio. Men in German Uniform: POWs in America during World War II. Knoxville: University of Tennessee Press, 2010.

Thompson, Glenn. Prisoners on the Plains: The German POW Camp at Atlanta. Holdrege, NE: Phelps County Historical Society, 1993.

"Throngs Expected to Greet Abbott, Costello in Appearance Here Friday for Bond Drive." Evening State Journal, July 30, 1942.

"TNT Poisoning at Mead Is 'Low.'" Omaha World-Herald, February 9, 1944.

Toft, Holly F. "All Out for Victory: The Nebraska Advisory Defense Committee in World War II." University of Nebraska–Kearney, 2017.

"12 Regional Defense Boards Selected." Lincoln Star, December 11, 1941.

"2,840,000 Was Mead's Total: Bomb Poundage Nearly Two Billion." Omaha World-Herald, August 26, 1945, Service edition.

Tysver, Robynn. "Kuroki Beat Bias to Serve with Distinction." Lincoln Journal Star, December 7, 1991.

"U. of N. Cannon to Join Scrap Drive." Lincoln Star, August 12, 1942.

"Unicameral: Defense Is Emphasized by Solons." Evening State Journal, February 11, 1941.

United Press. "Contracts for Bomber Plant at Omaha Signed." Nebraska State Journal, February 15, 1941.

———. "Isolationism of Midwest Believed Over-Emphasized." Lincoln Star, October 24, 1941.

———. "Lad Gets $5 from Letter to President." Nebraska State Journal, August 22, 1943.

———. "Nebraska Jap Promoted for Gunnery Skill." Omaha World-Herald, December 15, 1942.

———. "State Scrap Drive Hits 17 Million Pounds Collection." Nebraska State Journal, July 31, 1942.

Universal Press. "Platte Lad Sells Shirts for Canteen." Lincoln Journal, August 10, 1943.

UNK History Department. "About Kearney Army Air Field." Historic Kearney, March 1, 2016. https://historickearney.unk.edu.

"Urban League Girls Guests Kearney Base." Lincoln Star, July 26, 1943.

U.S. Air Force. "Bruning Air Base, Oct. 1942–Oct. 1948." U.S. government, 1948, 1942, RG538, roll no. 5, History Nebraska.

———. "Notes on the Earlier History of the Alliance Army Air Field." October 1944. RG538, Series 3, roll no. 4, History Nebraska.

———. "Scottsbluff Army Air Base, Jan. 1943–1944." 1944, 1943. RG538, rolls nos. 27 and 28, History Nebraska.

———. "Scribner Air Base, Feb. 1944–June 1945." 1945, 1944. RG 538, roll no. 28, History Nebraska.

"U.S.O. Coming to Lincoln 'in a Hurry,' Need Building like Rudge's, Says Finley." Evening State Journal, June 2, 1942.

"USO Discussion: Recreation Facilities Are Sifted at Meeting of Army with Navy Officials." Lincoln Star, November 28, 1944.

U.S. War Department. "Complete Report Covering Construction and Completion of Operational Training Unit, One Squadron Station, Ainsworth Satellite Field, Ainsworth, Nebraska, for Second Air Force." U.S. Army Corps of Engineers, December 31, 1942, History Nebraska.

———. "Handbook on Facilities of Posts, Camp, and Stations." 7th Service Command Publication, August 31, 1945. Camp Administration File. Fort Robinson Museum.

Village of Fairmont. "Fairmont Army Airfield." 2019. https://www.fairmont-nebraska.org.

"WAC Mess Hall Dressed Up with Colorful Paint, Drapes." The Duster 2, no. 16 (July 21, 1944).

"War Department Calls for Bids on Air Base." Evening State Journal, March 31, 1942.

"Welcome Sign Out at Hebron USO." Lincoln Star, September 26, 1943.

Wide World Press. "Business Today: Sugar Rationing." Lincoln Star, April 27, 1942.

Wit, Tracy Lynn. "The Social and Economic Impact of World War II Munitions Manufacture on Grand Island, Nebraska." Nebraska History 71 (1990): 151–63.

Yanik, Staff Sergeant Joe. "Off They Went…!!! AF's Women Airmen Raised the Bar." Air Force District of Washington, March 8, 2017. https://www.afdw.af.mil.

Yellin, Emily. Our Mothers' War: American Women at Home and at the Front during World War II. New York: Free Press, 2004.

ABOUT THE AUTHOR

N ebraska native Melissa A. Amateis grew up on a farm near Bridgeport, Nebraska. She holds a BA in history from Chadron State College and an MA in history from the University of Nebraska–Lincoln. Amateis lives with her daughter in eastern Nebraska. Follow her on Twitter at @WW2HistoryGal and visit her website at www.melissaamateis.com.